SO-CFM-459

THIS IS OUR FAITH

Series Authors: Janaan Manternach
Carl J. Pfeifer

Authors: Jacqueline Jambor
Joan R. DeMerchant
Maureen Gallagher

**Consulting
Editor:** Jean Marie Weber

Contributing Authors: Kate Sweeney Ristow
Sister Carolyn Puccio, C.S.J.

SILVER BURDETT GINN
PARSIPPANY, NJ

THIS IS OUR FAITH
SCHOOL PROGRAM

Contributing Authors: James Bitney, Robert Hamma, Paula A. Lenz, Judene Leon, Yvette Nelson, Sister Carolyn Puccio, C. S. J., Anna Ready, Kate Sweeney Ristow, Barbara Carol Vasiloff, Sister Maureen Shaughnessy, S.C., Sister Cecilia Maureen Cromwell, I.H.M., Patricia Frevert, Mary Lou Ihrig, Sister Arlene Pomije, C.S.J., Sister Mary Agnes Ryan, I.H.M., Brother Michael Sheerin, F.M.S.

Opening Doors: *A Take-Home Magazine:* Peter H.M. Demkovitz, Janie Gustafson, Margaret Savitskas

Day to Day: *Skills for Christian Living:* Susan G. Keys

Advisory Board:
Rev. Louis Camelli
Philip J. Cunningham
Sister Clare E. Fitzgerald
William J. Freburger
Greer J. Gordon
Sister Veronica R. Grover, S.H. C. J.
Rev. Thomas Guarino
Rev. Robert E. Harahan
Kathleen Hendricks
Rev. Eugene LaVerdierre, S.S.S.
Rev. Frank J. McNulty
Rev. Msgr. John J. Strynkowski

Consultants: Linda Blanchette, Anita Bridge, Fred Brown, Rod Brownfield, Sister Mary Michael Burns, S.C., Pat Burns, Bernadine Carroll, Mary Ellen Cocks, Sister Peggy Conlon, R.S.M., Mary Ann Crowley, Pamela Danni, Sister Jamesetta DeFelice, O.S.U., Sister Mary Elizabeth Duke, S.N.D., Mary M. Gibbons, Yolanda Gremillion, Sister Angela Hallahan, C.H.F., Alice T. Heard, Sister Michelle O'Connor, P.B.V.M., Sister Angela O'Mahoney, P.B.V.M., Sister Ruthann O'Mara, S.S.J., Sandra Okulicz-Hulme, Judy Papandria, Rachel Pasano, Sallie Ann Phelan, Sister Geraldine M. Rogers, S.S.J., Mary Lou Schlosser, Patricia Ann Sibilia, Margaret E. Skelley, Lisa Ann Sorlie, Sister Victorine Stoltz, O.S.B., Sister Nancy Jean Turner, S.H. C. J., Christine Ward, Judith Reidel Weber, Kay White, Elizabeth M. Williams, Catherine R. Wolf, Florence Bambrick Yarney, Kathryn K. Zapcic

Nihil Obstat
Kathleen Flanagan, S.C., Ph.D.
Censor Librorum
Ellen Joyce, S.C.
Censor Librorum

Imprimatur
✠ Most Reverend Frank J. Rodimer
Bishop of Paterson
November 22, 1996

The *nihil obstat* and *imprimatur* are official declarations that a book or pamphlet is free of doctrinal and moral error. No implication is declared therein that those who have granted the *nihil obstat* and *imprimatur* agree with the contents, opinions, or statements expressed.

Acknowledgments

Excerpts from the "Dogmatic Constitution on the Church (Lumen Gentium)" reprinted from *The Documents of Vatican II* by Walter M. Abbott, S.J. Copyright © 1966 by permission of New Century Publishers, Inc., Piscataway, New Jersey.

Scriptural text used in this work are taken from the *New American Bible with Revised New Testament* Copyright © 1970, 1986 by the Confraternity of Christian Doctrine, Washington, D.C. and are used by permission of copyright owner. All rights reserved.

All adaptations of Scripture are based on the *New American Bible with revised New Testament.*

Excerpts from the English translation of *Rite of Marriage* © 1969, International Committee on English in the Liturgy, Inc. (ICEL); excerpts from the English translation of *Rite of Baptism for Children* © 1969, ICEL; excerpts from the English translation of *The Roman Missal* ©1973, ICEL; excerpts from the English translation of *Rite of Penance* © 1974, ICEL; excerpts from the English translation of *Eucharistic Prayers for Masses with Children* © 1975, ICEL; excerpts from the English translation of *Rite for Confirmation*, Second Edition © 1975, ICEL; excerpts from *Pastoral Care of the Sick: Rites of Anointing and Viaticum* © 1982, ICEL; excerpts from the English translation of *Book of Blessings* © 1988, ICEL. All rights reserved.

Contents

LET US PRAY

Let Us Pray

The Lord's Prayer
Our Father, who art in heaven,
  hallowed be thy name;
thy kingdom come;
thy will be done on earth
  as it is in heaven.
Give us this day our daily bread;
and forgive us our trespasses
  as we forgive those
  who trespass against us;
and lead us not into temptation,
  but deliver us from evil.
Amen.

Padre Nuestro
Padre nuestro, que estás en el cielo,
  santificado sea tu nombre;
venga a nosotros tu reino;
hágase tu voluntad en la tierra
  como en el cielo.
Danos hoy nuestro pan de cada día;
perdona nuestras ofensas,
  como también nosotros
  perdonamos
  a los que nos ofenden;
no nos dejes caer en la tentación,
  y líbranos del mal.
Amén.

Sign of the Cross
In the name of the Father,
  and of the Son,
  and of the Holy Spirit.
Amen.

Señal de la Cruz
En el nombre del Padre,
  y del Hijo,
  y del Espíritu Santo.
Amén.

Hail Mary

Hail Mary, full of grace,
    the Lord is with you.
Blessed are you among women,
    and blessed is the fruit
    of your womb, Jesus.
Holy Mary, Mother of God,
    pray for us sinners, now,
    and at the hour of our death.
Amen.

Ave María

Dios te salve, María, llena eres de
    gracia,
    el Señor es contigo.
Bendita tú eres entre todas las
    mujeres,
    y bendito es el fruto
    de tu vientre, Jesús.
Santa María, Madre de Dios,
    ruega por nosotros, pecadores,
    ahora
    y en la hora de nuestra muerte.
Amén.

Glory Be to the Father

Glory be to the Father,
    and to the Son,
    and to the Holy Spirit.
As it was in the beginning,
    is now, and ever shall be,
    world without end.
Amen.

Gloria al Padre

Gloria al Padre,
    y al Hijo,
    y al Espíritu Santo.
Como era en el principio,
    ahora y siempre,
    por los siglos de los siglos.
Amén.

3

Let Us Pray

Grace Before Meals
Bless us, O Lord,
  and these your gifts,
  which we are about to receive
  from your goodness,
through Christ our Lord.
Amen.

Grace After Meals
We give you thanks
  for all your gifts,
  almighty God,
  living and reigning
  now and forever.
Amen.

A Morning Prayer
My God, I offer you today
  all I think and do and say,
  uniting it with what was
    done on earth,
by Jesus Christ, your Son.
Amen.

Evening Prayer
Dear God, before I sleep
  I want to thank you for this
  day
    so full of your kindness
    and your joy.
I close my eyes to rest safe
  in your loving care.
Amen.

Act of Contrition

My God,
I am sorry for my sins with all my heart.
In choosing to do wrong
and failing to do good,
I have sinned against you
whom I should love above all things.
I firmly intend, with your help,
to do penance,
and sin no more,
and to avoid whatever leads me to sin.
Our Savior Jesus Christ
suffered and died for us.
In his name, my God, have mercy.

(Revised Rite of Penance)

Prayer to the Holy Spirit

Come, Holy Spirit, fill the hearts of your
    faithful
and kindle in them the fire of your love.
Send forth your Spirit, and they shall be
    created;
and you will renew the face of the earth.
Amen.

Let us pray

Lord, by the light of the Holy Spirit
you have taught the hearts of your faithful.
In the same Spirit help us to relish what is
    right and always rejoice in your
    consolation. We ask this through Christ
    our Lord.
Amen.

Let Us Pray

The Apostles' Creed

I believe in God, the Father almighty,
    creator of heaven and earth;
I believe in Jesus Christ, his only Son,
    our Lord.
He was conceived by the power of the
    Holy Spirit and born of the Virgin Mary.
He suffered under Pontius Pilate, was
    crucified, died, and was buried.
He descended to the dead.
On the third day he rose again.
He ascended into heaven,
    and is seated at the right hand
    of the Father.
He will come again to judge the living
    and the dead.
I believe in the Holy Spirit,
    the holy catholic Church,
    the communion of saints,
    the forgiveness of sins,
    the resurrection of the body
    and life everlasting.
Amen.

Beginning the Journey

We are on our way to learn more about God, about ourselves, and about life. As we begin our journey this year, name some things you would like to know about your world, about yourself, and about God. Then list them on the lines below.

Things I would like to learn about my world.

1. _____

_____

2. _____

_____

Things I would like to learn about myself.

1. _____

_____

2. _____

_____

Things I would like to learn about God.

1. _____

_____

2. _____

_____

Prayer for the Journey

Leader: This is the Bible, the book of God's word. God speaks to us in the words of the Bible. We will keep the Bible with us throughout our journey of faith this year.

All: Your word, O Lord, is a lamp to guide me and a light on my path.

(Based on Psalm 119:105)

Leader: Let us listen to Jesus' promise to be with us on our way. No matter where we are, he is with us. Here are his words: "Behold, I am with you always" (based on Matthew 28:20).

All: Thanks be to God.

Leader: May God bless each of us as we begin our way together this year to learn more about ourselves and about God. May God bless these books, which we will use as our map along the way.

All: Amen!

THIS IS OUR FAITH

❋

A Preview of Grade 4

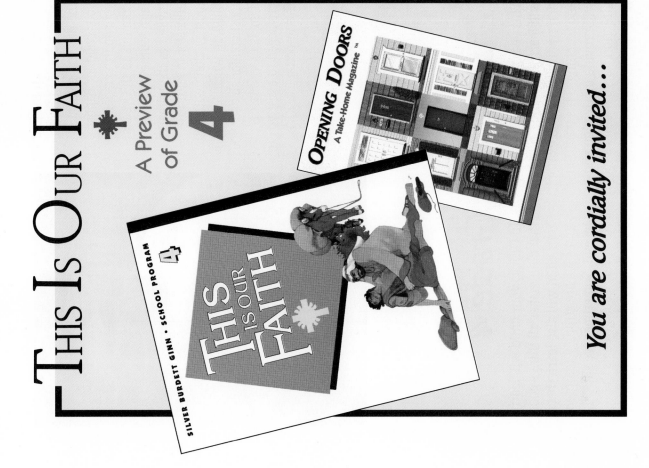

OPENING DOORS
A Take-Home Magazine ™

SILVER BURDETT GINN • SCHOOL PROGRAM 4

THIS IS OUR FAITH

You are cordially invited…

Profile of the Fourth-Grade Child

No one knows your child better than you! It may be helpful and interesting to you as a parent or guardian, however, to explore some of the characteristics of the fourth grader.

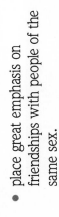

Fourth graders

- enjoy reading.

- learn readily from their observations.

- need parents' and other adults' warmth and support.

- need sets of guidelines and rules to follow.

- need to belong to a group, particularly an understanding family group.

- act more independently than when they were younger.

- place great emphasis on friendships with people of the same sex.

- like being and doing things with friends.

- have a general willingness to share with each other more than they did when they were younger.

THIS IS OUR FAITH Grade 4 Program has been designed to reflect the doctrine presented in the ***Catechism of the Catholic Church*** at a level that is appropriate for the fourth-grade child.

4

to continue on the journey of faith you first began on the day you presented your child for Baptism. As your fourth grader commits to this year's faith journey, you are invited as the primary educator in faith to journey along with your child, in whatever way is most comfortable for you. THIS IS OUR FAITH is privileged to assist you in this important task.

This Year in Grade 4

This year your fourth grader will learn about the Church's rich tradition of moral example and teaching. This tradition will provide motivation and direction for your child's moral growth. We begin the year with a look at Christian morality.

In Unit 1, your child will learn that God makes all things good. Your child will also learn that at times we are strongly tempted by evil. Sometimes we sin. However, Jesus gives us the Holy Spirit to help us choose good over evil.

As your child completes each unit of THIS IS OUR FAITH, you will receive *Opening Doors: A Take-Home Magazine.* Each magazine will include the following features to help you and your family share your faith.

A Closer Look

includes thought discussion starters, points for reflection, and an article relating the unit theme to a particular aspect of the Mass.

Being Catholic

explains a particular aspect of our Catholic heritage.

Growing Closer

suggests activities to help you and your family integrate your faith into everyday life.

And also . . .

Looking Ahead

A preview of the next unit of THIS IS OUR FAITH

UNIT 1

Choosing Between Good and Evil

What are some of the good things and bad things about our world?

Goodness from God

Activity

Write the names of some of the people, pets, foods, games, and places you see as good things in your life. Then draw in the space below a picture of one of your favorite things.

_____   _____

_____   _____

_____   _____

Who or what is the best gift in your life?

God's Gift of Goodness

Our world is filled with good people. It is filled with many gifts of God's creation. In the Bible we read about the goodness we see in each other. This goodness is God's gift to us, just as it was a gift to the people of long ago.

The Bible tells us that God creates everything that is good and makes people in his own image. The world is the Creator's gift to us. God gives the world to us to enjoy, to care for, and to use with respect. We are responsible for all living beings and the environment.

Activity

We are made in God's own image. With words or pictures, describe what God sees when he looks at you.

The Story of Creation

In the beginning, God spoke into the darkness. God said, "Let there be light," and there was light. God saw how good the light was.

Then God made the dome of sky. God gathered the waters below the sky into seas and oceans. Dry land appeared. God called the dry land "earth," and God was pleased.

Then God said, "Let the earth bring forth plants and flowers and trees." And the earth was filled with life and colors, with fruits and grains. God saw how good it was.

Then God set the sun in the sky to give light by day, and the moon and stars to shine upon the earth by night. God saw how good it was.

Then God said, "Let the waters be filled with living creatures and let birds fly in the sky." And so there were fish and birds of all kinds. God looked at them with great pleasure and blessed them all.

Then God said, "Let the earth be filled with every kind of animal." Animals both large and small, and tame and wild, began to move over the earth. And God saw how good it was.

And finally God said, "Let us make human beings in our own image and likeness to rule over the earth, the skies, and the seas." So God made a man and a woman who were very much like God.

God blessed the woman and man and said, "Have children who will live all over the earth. I am giving you and your children the whole world to care for, to use, and to enjoy."

God looked at everything and saw that it was all very good. So God stopped working and rested.

Based on Genesis 1:1—2:2

Activity

1. Name one part of God's creation that you think is most beautiful. Tell why.

_____

2. Name one animal for which you are particularly thankful. Tell why.

_____

3. God has given you some special people in your life. List as many as you can on the lines below.

_____   _____   _____

_____   _____   _____

_____   _____   _____

Activity

1. Name someone in your family who you think is a good person. _____

   Give an example of his or her goodness.

   _____

2. Name a friend who you think is a good person.

   _____

   Give an example of his or her goodness.

   _____

God's Grace

Everything that God makes is good. In creation the mountains, the seas, the animals, and especially people remind us of the Lord's goodness, love, and presence with us. God gives us people and things to help us be happy. God is present here with us in our world through people and all creation.

Catholics call God's loving presence in our lives **grace.**

Grace is a very special gift from God. Grace helps us see human beings and all of creation as holy and good. Grace gives us the strength to say no to selfishness and to act as the good people God created us to be. God's loving presence helps us choose what is good.

Activity

On the lines below, put a ✔ in front of the sentences below that show how you are a good person, filled with God's grace.

_____ I am generous.

_____ I get along well with others.

_____ I am cooperative in school.

_____ I am helpful at home.

_____ I tell the truth.

_____ I am a good friend.

_____ I respect people who are different from me.

_____ I remember to thank God in prayer.

_____ I invite others to be my friends.

_____ I encourage others when they need a kind word.

_____ I am kind to younger children.

_____ I respect my parents and teachers.

_____ I respect other people's property.

Vocabulary

grace: God's loving presence in our lives

● ● ● ● ● ● ● ● ● ●

We Believe

All that God makes is good and shows his goodness, love, and presence with us. God gives us people and things to help us be happy. The Lord is present here with us in our world. We call God's loving presence _grace._

A Prayer to Our Creator

Loving God, Creator of all life, thank you for giving me life and making me in your image and likeness. Thank you for the many ways you make your presence known to me. Your love fills my life, and I am thankful. Amen.

A Doer of Good Deeds

We can come to know God's love through the goodness of people and things in the world. A great Christian who saw the goodness of God in the people and things around him was Francis of Assisi.

Francis was born in Assisi, Italy, in 1182. Francis grew up to be a rich young man. He wanted to be a famous knight, who did great and noble deeds. One day, when Francis was dressed in a new uniform, he met a very poor man. Francis felt sorrow for the man, so he gave him his uniform.

On another day, Francis went to Rome, where he saw many beggars. He shared all his money with them. Soon Francis gave away everything—his money, his clothes, even his place in his father's house. Francis wanted only to do great and noble deeds for God. He wanted to be like Jesus.

Francis lived a simple, happy life, putting all his trust in God. He admired the simple life of the birds and other animals. He loved music and songs. He loved plants and flowers, so he had a beautiful garden.

Francis grew in his love for God. He also grew in his love for the goodness in people and things. Other people wanted to do great things for God, too. They began to follow Francis' example.

Today, Saint Francis of Assisi is one of the great saints of the Church. We celebrate his life and example on October 4.

Following Francis' Example

Just like Francis, we are called to care for all that God has given to us.

When we care for our world, we care for God's gift of creation. When we respect all living creatures, and care for animals we remember that they too are gifts from God.

We take care of the environment by not wasting our natural resources.

We care for God's great gift of people by respecting all people. We are called to be kind to others and to help those in need, just as Francis did.

Learning about Saint Francis helps us to know what to do to live as followers of Jesus.

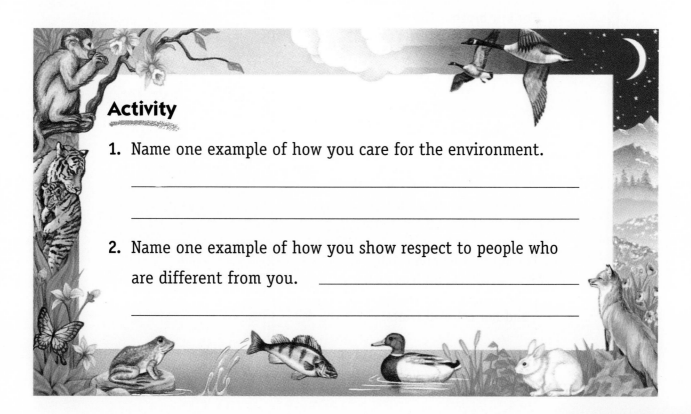

Activity

1. Name one example of how you care for the environment.

   _____

   _____

2. Name one example of how you show respect to people who are different from you. _____

   _____

Praying Prayers of Praise

The Church teaches us many different ways of praying. One kind of prayer is called *praise*. To praise someone means to tell the person how wonderful he or she is. We praise God for being wonderful. When we pray a prayer of praise, we can use joyful words, gestures, song, or even dance.

Saint Francis of Assisi was a person who often praised God. Pray this prayer of praise in a way that is comfortable for you. You might want to add gestures, dance steps, or music to the prayer.

Canticle of the Sun

Praise to you, Lord,
for our brother the sun,
beautiful and radiant;
by him you give us light.

For our brother the wind,
for the air and for the clouds,
for the clear sky,
and for every kind of weather.

For our sister the water.
She is so useful,
so precious, and so pure.

For our brother the fire,
who makes us warm;
by him you light up the night.

For our mother the earth,
who carries us and feeds us.
She gives us her plants
and her colorful fruits.

Praise to you, Lord, for all creatures.
Saint Francis of Assisi

Chapter Review

Read each statement below. Then write **true** or **false** on the line in front of each statement.

_____ **1.** God looked at all of creation and called it evil.

_____ **2.** God gives us the world to enjoy, to care for, and to use with respect.

_____ **3.** Francis was born in Germany in 1182.

_____ **4.** Francis lived a simple life, putting all his trust in God.

_____ **5.** God's presence in our lives is called responsibility.

Write the answers to the first two questions.

1. What is meant by God's *grace*?

_____

_____

2. What does the story of creation tell us about ourselves, about the world, and about God?

_____

_____

_____

_____

_____

All that the Lord has made is good.
Based on Sirach 39:33

3. Discuss how we can show thanks to God for so many gifts.

Evil in the World

I Don't Understand

One day, Jason was thinking to himself, "I don't understand something. Why is it that I can do kind and loving things for others and feel happy one day and then another day I can be so unkind and feel like this—alone and sad? How can I have both good feelings and bad feelings in me?"

Jason continued thinking, "Then I look at our world. Lots of people are doing good, loving things for others, while other people are starting wars, selling drugs, and polluting our lakes and rivers. It seems that we live in a world that is good, but there is evil in it, too. Even in our hearts, goodness and sinfulness are mixed. We can love and hate, and help and hurt."

Discuss

Do you ever feel the same way that Jason feels?

Think of a time when you were hurting about something. How did you feel? What did you do to feel better?

Goodness and Evil

How do we know when something is evil? We can recognize evil in the world because evil is hurtful to others. Evil causes suffering and pain. Evil is always wrong and harmful. Evil tries to destroy what is good.

How do we know when something is good? Goodness causes happiness and peace. Goodness is choosing what is right and loving. All good people and good things can remind us of God.

Activity

Rearrange the letters in the words below to name different kinds of good and evil. The first letter of each word has been underlined for you.

KINDS OF GOOD

1. ove<u>l</u> _____

2. gessnor<u>f</u>ive _____

3. p<u>h</u>el _____

4. s<u>c</u>oonmasip _____

5. ca<u>p</u>ee _____

6. meli<u>s</u> _____

KINDS OF EVIL

1. ar<u>w</u> _____

2. su<u>a</u>be _____

3. grune<u>h</u> _____

4. at<u>h</u>e _____

5. lu<u>p</u>intool _____

6. jd<u>p</u>eeicru _____

A Beautiful Garden

God created man and woman and loved them. They lived in a beautiful garden. The woman and the man loved each other and were very happy. They loved the fish in the streams, the birds in the sky, and all the other animals. They loved and enjoyed the flowers and plants in God's garden. But there was one tree in the garden that God told the woman and man not to touch.

One day the Tempter appeared and asked the woman, "Did God really tell you not to eat the fruit of any of the trees in the garden?"

"No," the woman answered. "God told us not to eat the fruit of only one tree in the whole garden. God said that if we ate its fruit, we would die."

"You won't die," the Tempter said. "God knows that if you eat the fruit of that tree, you will be like gods. You will know good from evil."

The woman looked at the tree. It was beautiful and full of fruit. She took some of the fruit and ate it. She gave some fruit to the man, and he ate it, too. Suddenly the man and woman felt ashamed.

That evening, God was moving about in the cool garden. The woman and man hid.

But God saw them and asked, "Why did you eat fruit from the tree?"

"The woman gave me some fruit, so I ate it," the man said.

"The Tempter tricked me, so I ate the fruit," the woman told the Lord.

"Because you disobeyed and did this evil thing," God said, "you will know suffering and pain. Your work will be hard, and you will become very tired. Thorns and weeds will grow from the earth. And you will die." Then God told the man and the woman that they must leave the garden.

Based on Genesis 2:8–3:23

Evil in the World

God made everyone and everything good. But we know from our experience that there is now evil mixed with good in all of creation. The Bible shows that evil comes not from God but from people's selfish choices. Sinful choices have **consequences**.

Sin spreads through the selfish actions of people. The Church calls the first selfish act **original sin**. It touches all of us who are born into a world hurt by evil.

Vocabulary

consequences: the things that follow from a choice or an action

original sin: the first selfish act of the first human beings, and the sinful condition into which we are born

We Believe

The goodness of the world is spoiled by sin. Sin is part of each one of us. It has been part of the world since God's first people began to act selfishly. This first selfish act is called *original sin*.

A Parish Community Brings God's Goodness

Resurrection Parish is a parish community in Oregon where all the parishioners of every age work together to overcome the evils that can be part of life today.

Adults at Resurrection Parish bring food and serve dinner to homeless people at a city shelter, and parish teenagers travel every summer to help repair and rebuild homes for families in need.

The fourth graders at Resurrection Parish have their own special project. They collect warm coats every year so that homeless and needy families will have warm clothing for the cold Oregon winters. One year the students collected more than 400 coats.

Every year the children of the parish gather school supplies and clothing to be taken to children in a mission parish in West Virginia. Even the very young children do their share of bringing goodness to God's people by bringing donated fruit juice to a local hospice.

By working together, the people of Resurrection Parish are fighting against evil in the world and bringing goodness to the people of God.

Activity

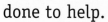

The pictures show examples of evil that people can do something about. On the lines beside each picture, write what could be done to help.

_____

_____

_____

_____

_____

_____

_____

_____

_____

_____

_____

_____

_____

_____

What One Person Can Do

God calls us to fight against all kinds of evil in ourselves and in our world. A great Christian who did just that was Saint Martin de Porres.

Martin was born in 1579. He lived in Lima, Peru, in South America. His father, a white Spaniard, did not want Martin because he was black like his mother. So Martin's mother took care of him by herself.

Even as a child, Martin could understand the sufferings of poor people. He gave them money and food.

As a teenager, Martin often cared for sick people. Later Martin joined a group of men called Dominican friars. Together they cared for sick priests and brothers. Rich people gave Martin medicine, food, and clothing, which he then gave to the poor.

Martin built a place for the poor children of Lima to live. He even built a school for them.

Martin took special care of the slaves who were brought to Peru. Martin became famous throughout Lima. About 300 years after Martin's death, Pope John XXIII named him a saint.

Making a Difference

Most of the time we hear how groups of people are making a difference in our world. Yet often it is one person alone who takes the first step toward fighting evil. Saint Martin de Porres is a good example of what one person can do. Following Jesus' example, Martin began his work alone but was soon joined by others. Martin used the gifts and talents that God gave him to help others. His goodness helped overcome the hurt and suffering of many people.

Each of us has been given gifts and talents. Each of us can share our goodness with others. Alone or joined with others, we can each make a difference in the lives of people who are hurting.

Activity

Think of one person you know who is hurting. Write one thing you can do for that person to ease his or her hurt.

_____

_____

Praying Spontaneously

One of the most wonderful things about prayer is that it can happen anywhere and at any time. We can pray at mealtimes and before going to sleep. We can gather with our families and with our school and parish communities for special times of prayer.

Spontaneous prayer is different. *Spontaneous* means "on the spur of the moment; without planning." By learning how to pray spontaneously, we can remember that God is always near us, in good times and in bad times. When we pray on the spur of the moment, we can have an ongoing conversation with God.

These fourth graders want to share with you how they pray spontaneously.

Teresa (Fairbanks, Alaska): Whenever I think about my dog Snowball and my cat Clancy while I'm at school I pray, "Thanks, God, for giving me Snowball and Clancy. Keep them safe and happy until I get home."

Ricardo (Brownsville, Texas): Sometimes I see homeless people on the streets. I pray, "God, it hurts me to see these people living on the streets. Please take care of them."

Kerry (Boston, Massachusetts): My mom taught me to say a little prayer each time I see an ambulance. I pray, "Dear God, please be with the person who is sick or injured, and be with those who are caring for the sick person."

If you could pray a spontaneous prayer right now, what would it be?

Chapter Review

On the lines below, list five evils that cause suffering in our world. Then on the lines next to each evil named, tell what could be done to fight against the evil.

1. _____   _____
                               _____

2. _____   _____
                               _____

3. _____   _____
                               _____

4. _____   _____
                               _____

5. _____   _____
                               _____

Write the answers to the first two questions.

1. What is meant by *original sin*?

   _____

   _____

   _____

2. When did evil in the world begin?

   _____

   _____

Turn from evil, and do good.
Psalm 34:15

3. Discuss how evil in the world hurts each one of us and the world itself.

Choices to Make

Sarah's Temptation

Sarah's mom asked Sarah to go with her to the mall. "You need new jeans," she said. "You can invite a friend if you want."

Sarah invited Jenny, who said she could be ready in fifteen minutes. It was always fun to go to the mall.

When they got to the mall, they looked at jeans and jackets, but Sarah's eyes were drawn to a headband in the next aisle. When her mom was not looking, Sarah whispered to Jenny, "I just love that headband! I want it, but I know my mom won't buy it for me."

Jenny glanced over at the headbands. She noticed that no one was working behind the counter. A couple of minutes later, she whispered back to Sarah, "While your mom is paying for your jeans, let's take a couple of headbands. They're cool. Nobody will see us."

How do you choose between right and wrong?

Sarah's mom looked at her watch. "It's getting late," she said, "I'll pay for the jeans."

"We'll stay right here," Sarah said. "Jenny wants to look at more jeans."

Sarah's mom agreed, since the cash register was close by and the store was almost empty.

"Now's our chance," Jenny said, tugging on Sarah's arm. "Your mom has her back to us. In two seconds the headbands will be ours."

Sarah thought for a second longer and then she

_____

_____

_____

_____

_____

Temptation in Our Lives

Everyone is tempted. We are tempted when something that we know is wrong looks very inviting to us. We may be drawn to act in a way that is wrong, or we may be tempted to say something we know is wrong. We may even find that we are attracted to people who always seem to get into trouble.

A **temptation** is an attraction to think, say, or do something we know is wrong. When we are tempted, we are *attracted* to do something wrong.

Everyone is tempted at some time to think, say, or do things that are wrong. Even Jesus was tempted. Jesus fought against his temptations. With his help, we can, too.

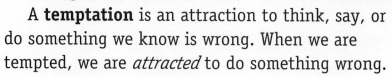

Vocabulary

temptation: an attraction to think, say, or do something we know is wrong

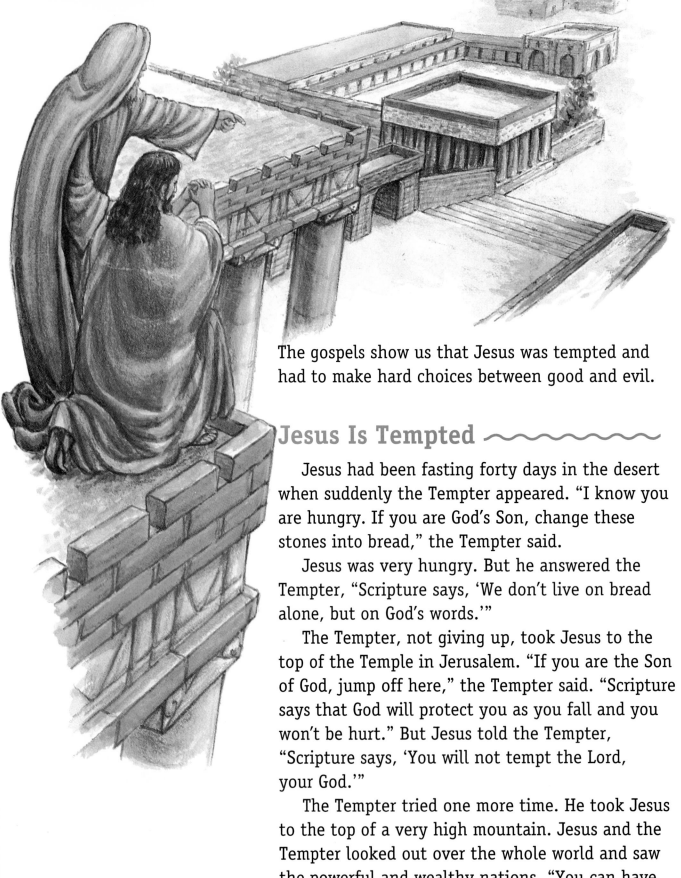

The gospels show us that Jesus was tempted and had to make hard choices between good and evil.

Jesus Is Tempted

Jesus had been fasting forty days in the desert when suddenly the Tempter appeared. "I know you are hungry. If you are God's Son, change these stones into bread," the Tempter said.

Jesus was very hungry. But he answered the Tempter, "Scripture says, 'We don't live on bread alone, but on God's words.'"

The Tempter, not giving up, took Jesus to the top of the Temple in Jerusalem. "If you are the Son of God, jump off here," the Tempter said. "Scripture says that God will protect you as you fall and you won't be hurt." But Jesus told the Tempter, "Scripture says, 'You will not tempt the Lord, your God.'"

The Tempter tried one more time. He took Jesus to the top of a very high mountain. Jesus and the Tempter looked out over the whole world and saw the powerful and wealthy nations. "You can have all that," the Tempter said to Jesus, "if only you bow down and worship me."

Jesus answered, "Go away! Scripture says, 'You will only worship the Lord, your God.'"

The Tempter left as suddenly as he had come. Jesus had overcome the temptations.

Based on Matthew 4:1–11

Activity

The Tempter wanted Jesus to use his power in wrong ways. What were the three temptations that Jesus faced?

1. _____

2. _____

3. _____

Jesus used strong words to answer the Tempter. Give an example of some words you might use when you are tempted.

_____

_____

Temptation and Sin

Our world is good, but evil hurts it. Though we are made like God, we feel the effects of original sin.

We are called to love God as we love ourselves and to love all people and things around us. But sometimes something can seem so good that we will do anything to get it. We become willing to do what we know is wrong, and we act selfishly. When we choose in this way to turn away from God, we **sin**. When we sin we are choosing not to love, or we are failing to do what we know we should do.

Temptation is not a sin. Jesus was tempted, as we are, but he never sinned. He chose never to turn away from God or God's way of life.

Activity

Mark each of the following with a **T** if you think the person was only tempted. Mark each with an **S** if you think the person might have sinned.

_____ Rebecca got an F on her report card. She thought about lying to her parents about it but changed her mind.

_____ Roberto's teacher was sick at home with the flu. Roberto was extremely disruptive in class, making it very difficult for his classmates to learn or for the substitute teacher to teach.

_____ At the store, Mark took some candy bars when the clerk wasn't looking.

_____ A girl at school continued to make fun of Shamina. Shamina thought about calling the girl some bad names to get back at her. She decided to walk away.

_____ Tong's brother accidentally gave him a bloody nose when they were fooling around. Tong was ready to hit him back to get even. Tong stopped for a minute and decided not to hit his brother.

Give one example of a temptation.

_____

_____

Give one example of a sin.

_____

_____

Vocabulary

sin: to choose to act selfishly; to turn away from God and choose not to love; to fail to do something we know we should do

We Believe

We are all tempted. Jesus was tempted, just as we are. Temptation is not a sin. We sin only when we choose to give in to temptation and turn away from God. With Christ's help, we can overcome temptation.

Freedom to Choose

One of the gifts God has given us is our freedom to choose. We can choose good instead of evil, and we can choose right instead of wrong. As we grow up, we will be able to make more and more choices for ourselves.

Even though God gives us freedom to choose, rules can guide our choices. For instance, our government gives us rules called laws. These laws are meant to keep us safe in our communities.

Our families also give us rules to live by because they love us. These rules are meant to keep us safe and happy and to help us make good choices.

Out of love for us, God also gives us rules that affect our freedom to choose. In the next weeks and months, we will learn more about God's rules.

Because we have the freedom to make choices, we can always be tempted to make the wrong choices. So as we grow and are able to make more choices for ourselves, we need to be ready to face temptations. When faced with temptation we can make good choices. We can choose to ask someone to help us. We can turn our attention away from the temptation and toward other things. We can also choose to remember that Jesus is with us.

Activity

Look carefully at the photograph. Imagine yourself as the person being tempted. Think about how you feel, what you are drawn to, what you want, and what you could do. Then write two story maps, one in which you give in to temptation and the other in which you overcome it. In both story maps, write the outcomes of your choices and actions.

Say YES to Drugs

Say NO to Drugs

Praying the Psalms

People of the Jewish and Christian faiths have been praying the psalms for thousands of years. The psalms are prayer songs that were written for many different occasions and reasons. They were probably used most often when Jews gathered to pray at the Temple in Jerusalem.

We hear a psalm sung during the Liturgy of the Word each Sunday. We call it the Responsorial Psalm.

Singing the psalms is only one way psalms can be prayed. We can pray the psalms by

- memorizing a few lines of a favorite psalm and praying the words over and over.

- joining others and reading the psalm aloud; taking turns reading the verses.

- choosing a psalm to pray for a specific reason, such as Psalm 43: A Prayer to God in Time of Trouble.

The psalm below is a psalm that asks God's help in overcoming temptation. Pray it in a way that is most comfortable for you. You might want to copy the psalm onto a small index card and place it where you will see it often.

Lord, be with me and help me,
for I must choose.
Be with me and help me.

Based on Psalm 22:11,19

Chapter Review

Look at the picture. Write the answers to the questions below.

1. What is the person being tempted to do?

_____

2. How can this person overcome temptation?

_____

_____

My dad said I have to finish my job.

What are you waiting for? Let's go!

Write the answers to the first two questions.

1. What is the difference between temptation and sin?

_____

_____

2. How can we know that we can overcome temptation?

_____

_____

_____

3. Discuss some ways in which we can fight against temptation.

God says, "I give you a choice between good and evil. Choose to follow my ways." Based on Deuteronomy 30:19 – 20

4 Choosing What Is Good

Activity

The children skateboarding in the picture above are making choices about the girl who wants to join them. What kinds of choices are the children making? Label each child with a word that describes his or her choice.

Our Conscience Can Help

Choosing can be difficult. But our **conscience**, or power to judge between good and bad, can help us. It is not always easy to choose what we know is good. We may be very sure of what we should do, but we still might find it hard to do. Sometimes we want to do what we know is wrong. In spite of our conscience, we decide that we don't want to choose what is good.

Activity

A TV reporter met people passing by on a busy street corner. The question she asked each person was this: "Why do you think people sometimes choose to do what is wrong?"

Here are some answers.

- "Probably they think their friends will laugh at them if they choose what is right."

- "Because they didn't think they would ever get caught."

- "People will do just about anything for money."

- "It feels good. It's fun."

Write your answer on the lines below.

_____

_____

_____

_____

_____

_____

Vocabulary

conscience: our power to judge whether something is good or bad

The Story of Pentecost ~~~~~

It was a quiet morning in Jerusalem fifty days after Jesus died and was risen from the dead. Jesus' friends were together in a house. They locked the doors. They were afraid that if they went out into the streets they would be caught and killed, as Jesus had been. They prayed very hard.

Suddenly there was a noise. It sounded like a strong wind blowing all through the house. The friends saw flames that looked like tongues of fire moving around the room. The flames came to rest above each of Jesus' friends.

Jesus' friends felt stronger and braver. Their fears seemed to disappear. They smiled as peace began to fill their hearts. Jesus' friends unlocked the doors. They went out to do what they had been afraid to do. They told everyone about Jesus. They knew that it was the Holy Spirit, promised by Jesus, who gave them their new courage, peace, and joy.

Based on Acts 2:1–4.

The Gift of the Holy Spirit

When Jesus had difficult choices to make, he did not turn away from God's love. Through the power of the Holy Spirit, Jesus overcame temptation. He promised to give us the Holy Spirit. The Holy Spirit comes to help and guide us in our fight against temptation, just as he first came to Jesus' followers on Pentecost.

Two Brave Women

It was the year 203 A.D. Two young women, Perpetua and Felicity, had a choice to make. And they had the Holy Spirit to help them make it.

Perpetua and Felicity were put in prison because they wanted to become Christians. The two women were afraid in the hot, dark prison. They feared they would be beaten and killed. They prayed for God's help.

Then Perpetua and Felicity were baptized. The Holy Spirit brought them great peace. They were no longer frightened.

Later the prison guards led Perpetua and Felicity outside to meet a judge. "Turn away from Jesus and worship our god," the judge ordered, "or I will have you killed."

The two women saw soldiers pacing back and forth, waiting to kill them with swords.

"No!" Perpetua said to the judge. "We will never turn away from Jesus."

"Let them die!" the judge ordered.

The two Christians hugged each other as the soldiers charged at them. Perpetua and Felicity were very brave as they faced death. The Church calls them saints and martyrs. We celebrate their feast on March 7.

Discuss

1. Why were the women in this story put in prison?
2. What temptation did the two women face?
3. What happened to them because of their decision?

Signs of the Spirit

Jesus gives us the same Holy Spirit he gave to his friends on Pentecost and to Perpetua and Felicity. We celebrate this gift in each of the seven sacraments. The Holy Spirit is always with us to help us and guide us in our fight against temptation. With the Holy Spirit we can know what is good. We can choose good and turn away from what is evil. In this way we will love God and all the goodness around us.

Christians have come to recognize signs that remind us that the Holy Spirit is with us, guiding us to make good choices. The Bible names nine signs:

love	generosity
joy	faithfulness
peace	gentleness
patience	self-control
kindness	*Based on Galatians 5:22 – 23*

Activity

Study the photograph on this page. Then on the lines below, name the signs of the Holy Spirit that the photograph suggests.

_____

_____

_____

_____

We Believe

Jesus sends us the Holy Spirit to be our helper and guide in our fight against temptation. The Holy Spirit helps us know what is good for us. The Holy Spirit guides us in choosing good rather than evil.

How to Make a Good Choice

The Holy Spirit helps us to be wise, strong, and caring so that we can make the right choices. Here are some steps to help you choose to do what is good when you feel drawn to do what is wrong.

▲ 1. **Stop** for a moment. Hold back from acting too quickly.

▲ 3. **Pray** and ask the Holy Spirit to help you make a good choice.

▲ 2. **Think** for a moment: Why do I want to do what I know is wrong? What will happen if I choose to do what I know is wrong? How will I feel? What would my parents and best friends think?

▲ 4. **Ask** someone you love and trust to tell you what he or she thinks is the right choice.

◄ 5. **Choose** to do what you think is the right thing to do.

Activity

Imagine that last summer you had a job doing yardwork for an elderly man. Each Saturday you rode your bike a mile to his house. The man could hardly walk and couldn't see very well. He always seemed to be in a bad mood and was never very nice to you. But you still liked the job because each week the man paid you six dollars.

Every Saturday the man would pay you with a $5 bill and a $1 bill. On the last Saturday of the summer, when you got home, you realized that the man had paid you with a $5 bill and a $20 bill by mistake. Instead of paying you six dollars, he paid you twenty-five dollars! What should you do? Complete the sentences below.

1. I would STOP and

2. I would THINK

3. I would PRAY. I would ask the Holy Spirit to

4. I would ASK

5. The CHOICE I would make would be to

Praying a Traditional Prayer

The Church has prayed certain prayers for hundreds of years. We call these prayers and other long-prayed prayers *traditional prayers*. Every generation of Catholics has learned and prayed these prayers. Your parents and grandparents have prayed them, and someday your children and grandchildren will pray the same prayers.

You already know some traditional prayers prayed by Catholics. The Lord's Prayer, the Hail Mary, and the Glory Be to the Father are traditional prayers.

Learn to pray this traditional prayer called the Act of Love.

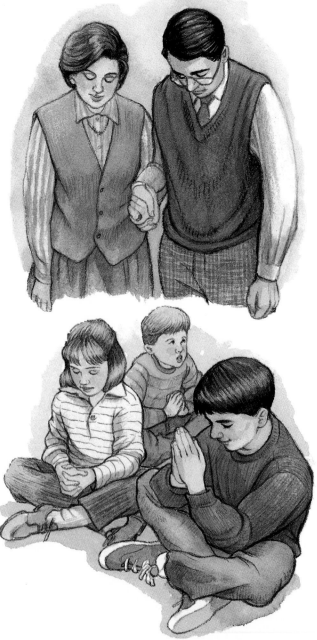

Act of Love

O my God, I love you above all things, with my whole heart and soul, because You are all–good and worthy of all love. I love my neighbor as myself for the love of You. I forgive all who have injured me, and I ask pardon of all whom I have injured. Amen.

Chapter Review

Put the steps of decision making in the correct order by numbering the statements from 1 through 5.

Ask someone you love and trust to tell you what he or she thinks is the the right choice.

Think for a moment: What will happen if I choose to do what I know is wrong?

Stop for a moment. Hold back from acting too quickly.

Choose to do what you think is the right thing to do.

Pray. Ask the Holy Spirit to help you make a good choice.

Write the answers to the first two questions.

1. What is meant by *conscience?* _____

_____

_____

2. How do we know that the Holy Spirit is with us to help us and guide us in making good choices?

_____

_____

The Spirit that God has given us makes us strong, loving, and wise.
Based on
2 Timothy 1:7

3. Discuss how we can find help to choose good rather than evil.

UNIT 1 ORGANIZER

Choosing Between Good and Evil

Chapter 1

List some signs of God's goodness.

Goodness from God

Chapter 2

Some examples of how we can fight against evil are

Evil in the World

Chapter 3

List some examples of temptation fourth graders might face.

Choices to Make

Chapter 4

You might need to listen to your conscience when

Choosing What Is Good

UNIT **1** REVIEW

Match the words in Column A with the definitions in Column B.

Column A

1. grace
2. original sin
3. temptation
4. sin
5. conscience

Column B

_____ to choose to act selfishly; to turn away from God and choose not to love

_____ God's gift of his own life and presence to people

_____ our power to judge whether something is good or bad

_____ the first selfish act and the sinful condition in which we are born

_____ an attraction to think, say, or do something we know is sinful

Fill in the word(s) that best completes each sentence. You may use a word more than once.

| evil | helper | love | Pentecost | God | Tempter |
| goodness | guide | unselfishness | | people | temptation |

1. All that God makes is good and shows God's

   _____ and _____ .

2. _____ spreads through the selfish actions of _____ .

3. We sin only when we choose to give in to _____

   and turn away from _____ .

4. The Holy Spirit first came to Jesus' followers on _____ .

5. Jesus sends us the Holy Spirit to be our _____ and _____ .

6. One of the signs of the Holy Spirit is _____ .

7. The _____ asked Jesus to bow down and worship him.

UNIT 1 REVIEW

List the three temptations that Jesus faced.

1. _____

2. _____

3. _____

Complete the word puzzle by filling in the blanks and then using the words to work the puzzle.

Across

3. _____ is one of the signs of the Holy Spirit.

4. Some _____ we make are good and some are bad.

7. Our _____ is the power to judge whether something is good or bad for us.

Down

1. A strong _____ seemed to blow through the house where Jesus' friends were.

2. The Holy Spirit first came to Jesus' friends on _____ .

3. On Pentecost, _____ that looked like tongues of fire seemed to come to rest above each of Jesus' friends.

5. Jesus gives us the Holy _____ to be our helper and our guide.

6. Like _____ we also have difficult choices to make.

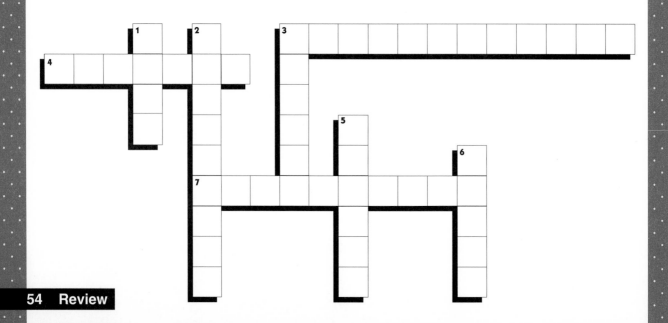

CELEBRATING MY CHRISTIAN IDENTITY

Jesus calls us to be his followers. As followers of Jesus we try to live our lives as Jesus lived his. We try to act in ways that are loving. We do this by being kind to others, treating others fairly, and by thinking of others' needs before our own.

Activity

For each of the stories that follow, tell if you think the main character is acting like a follower of Jesus.

Story #1

Tonya's little sister asks Tonya if she can play with Tonya and her friend. At first Tonya says no because she doesn't like having her sister tag along when she has a friend over after school. Then Tonya thinks about how unhappy her sister seems at having to play alone, and Tonya asks her friend if it's okay for her sister to play with them. Is Tonya acting like a follower of Jesus?

Yes   No

Story #2

Jim's brother's bike is in the shop for repairs. Jim's brother wants to go on a bike ride with his friends, and asks Jim if he can borrow his bike. Jim says no. Is Jim acting like a follower of Jesus?

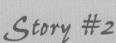

Yes   No

Story #3

Jason's best friend asks to copy Jason's homework. Jason feels uncomfortable about giving it to him and says no. Jason offers to help his friend with the homework if there was something his friend didn't understand. Is Jason acting like a follower of Jesus?

Yes　　　　　　　　　　**No**

Story #4

Kate is mad at Jonna because Jonna wouldn't play with her at recess. Jonna apologizes, but Kate turns her back and refuses to hear what Jonna has to say. Is Kate acting like a follower of Jesus?

Yes　　　　　　　　**No**

Activity

Write a story that tells about a time when being a follower of Jesus was difficult for you.

_____

_____

_____

_____

_____

_____

_____

_____

_____

PRAYER

Jesus, I want to live my life as you lived yours. Help me to be kind to others and to think of others' needs before my own. Amen.

OPENING DOORS
A Take-Home Magazine™

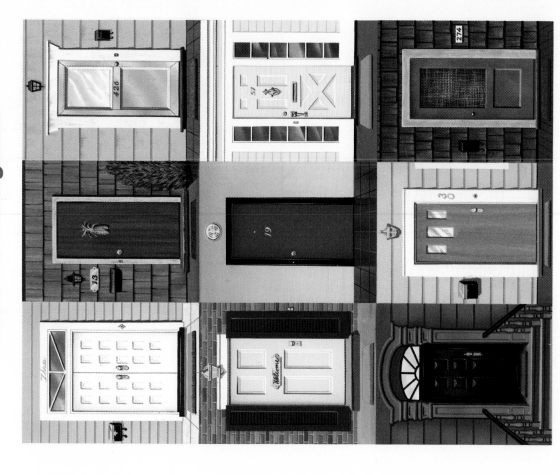

Growing Closer

MAKE A WEATHER-REPORT flip chart to display in your kitchen. The poster will chart what the communication climate is like in your home. You may want to use the illustrations on page 3 of this booklet. A sample illustration is provided.

Looking Ahead

Unit 2 will present the Christian way of love, mercy, and justice as formulated in the Great Commandment, the Beatitudes, and the Ten Commandments and as lived out by Jesus, the saints, and faithful Christians today. Your fourth grader will learn that these teachings of Jesus should be the guidelines for his or her life, too.

CLIMATE CONTROL

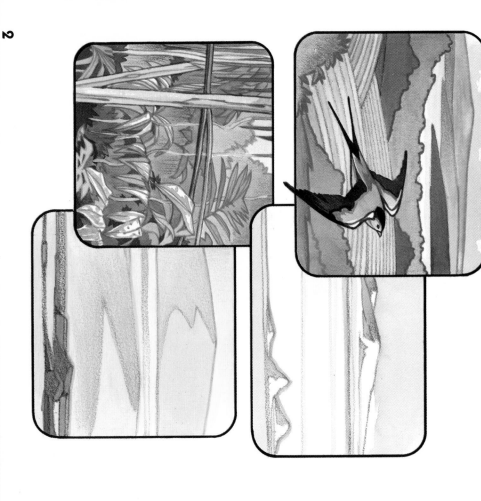

Some parishes offer family evening programs that focus on the family in its home setting. The family studies and discusses a designated topic, then completes a common activity.

• **Child-centered parish programs.** Most religion textbooks used today in parochial schools and in parish schools of religion contain suggested family activities. By completing these activities with your child, you can take an active part in your child's religious education. You can also further your own religious education.

• **Sunday liturgies.** Attending Mass with your child, reading together the Scripture readings before Mass, and discussing the homily after Mass can be excellent ways to share your faith as a family.

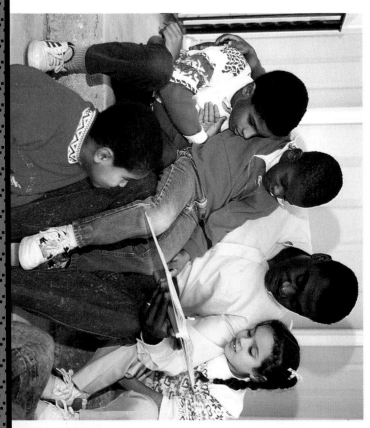

TRANSMITTING THE FAITH

Recent research reports about the religious formation of children emphasize the vital nurturing role of the family and supporting role of the Church community.

The National Catholic Educational Association (NCEA) study, *Toward Effective Parish Religious Education for Children and Young People*, states, "Without faith-supporting activities at home, many youth fall prey to a religious skepticism that grows and festers. When parents are seen as mechanical religionists who practice the faith only at Mass, adolescents tend to learn that faith is an adult game that really has no important tie to work or family or life decisions. The family that practices faith models a mature faith, and the message does not escape our children."

Sharing the Light of Faith, National Catechetical Directory for Catholics of the United States states, "Within families there is need and opportunity for spouses to catechize each other and for parents to catechize children."

Most parishes are ready to support family efforts. The following ways describe how your family can transmit your faith to or catechize each other.

- **Parish family-centered programs.** Many parishes offer family-centered religious education programs. In some programs, the participants separate into age groups to discuss a scriptural topic or liturgical theme. Then everyone participates in a common activity and celebration.

At any given time, the climate of communication in your home may be like one or two listed below.

People are barely speaking to each other. One person has decided to give everyone else the cold shoulder.

People are listless. Everyone is exhausted. They do not have the energy or desire to improve the level of conversation.

There are a few hot family issues that need to be discussed. However, someone is retreating to a little oasis.

TEMPERATE

Everyone is mellow. People are really expressing themselves calmly. Each person is participating in the conversation at the breakfast or dinner table.

- If you feel your family is experiencing an Arctic, tropical, or desert climate, what can you do to improve the atmosphere?

- If your family is experiencing a temperate climate, what can you do to maintain the pleasant atmosphere?

TURNING OFF and TUNING IN

What kind of energy does your family generate as you are getting ready for Mass each week? Take a few minutes to discuss this question with your family.

Sometimes your energy may be spent as you all rush about in a whirlwind getting dressed and piling into the car. During these times, you may feel like a tornado picked you up from your house and then plopped you into the middle of the church just as the entrance song begins. At other blessed times, you may have a few minutes of peace—a few minutes to turn off all sources of distraction from the previous week.

To help you turn off distracting waves of worry, planning, and the rehashing of situations, we pray together the Opening Prayer before the Liturgy of the Word begins. The priest invites us to pray, pauses for a few minutes of silence, and then begins the prayer, which is also known as the Collect.

The prayer below is the Alternative Opening Prayer for the Twenty-First Sunday in Ordinary Time. Find a few minutes to reflect on the meaning of the words during the coming week.

Lord our God,
all truth is from you,
and you alone bring oneness of heart.
Give your people the joy
of hearing your word in every sound
and of longing for your presence more
than for life itself.
May all the attractions of a changing world
serve only to bring us
the peace of your kingdom which this
world does not give.

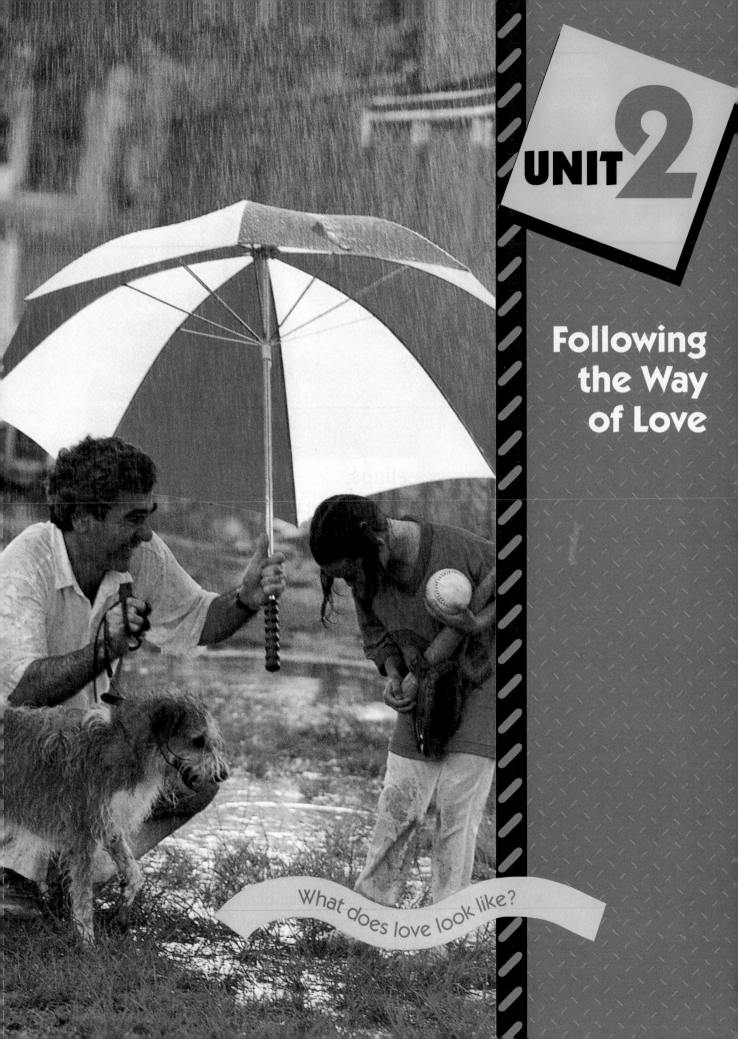

UNIT 2

Following the Way of Love

What does love look like?

The Great Commandment

What are some reasons why people help those who are hurting?

Mixed Feelings

"Jesse! It's time to get up!"

Jesse rolled over. "I'm tired," he called back to his mother. He pulled the covers over his head.

Five minutes later, Jesse's sister came into his room. "Jesse," she said, "we have to hurry. It's our day to help out at the soup kitchen."

Jesse did not want to hear about poor people. He knew they would already be lined up in the cold outside the soup kitchen door. He wanted to stay in his warm, cozy bed.

"Let's go!" Jesse could hear his father say. "You're going to be late."

Jesse did not answer. "Those men and women lined up for food won't miss me," he thought. "Mom, Dad, and Kate can feed them. I'll just go back to sleep."

But he couldn't sleep. Jesse could hear his parents and sister packing boxes and getting ready. Restless, he wondered what it would be like not to have enough to eat.

"Well, it's not my fault if people are hungry," he thought to himself.

He was just dozing off when his dad came into his room and sat down on his bed. "Son, we have to leave in a few minutes. It's cold outside. Those people are already standing in the cold and are hungry. Your grandma is staying home. She has a bad cold. So you can stay in bed if you want, or you can go with us. If you decide to go, you have to be in the car in ten minutes."

His dad left the room. Jesse tossed and turned for a minute before deciding what to do.

Jesus' Great Commandment

Jesus teaches us to love God above all else and to love our **neighbor** as we love ourselves. This teaching is called Jesus' Great **Commandment**. For Jesus, our neighbor is the person who lives in our homes, in our neighborhoods, or in a country far away. Our neighbor is the person who sits next to us in school or who plays soccer on our team. Our neighbor is every man, woman, and child, especially anyone who is hurting and needs our love and care. Caring for our neighbor is how we best show our love for God.

Activity

List some things that people need in your home, in your school, and in your neighborhood.

_____

_____

_____

Vocabulary

neighbor: every man, woman, and child, especially someone who needs our love and care

commandment: a law given to us by God to help us live good lives by being loving people

/////////////////

We Believe

Jesus teaches us to love God above all else and to love our neighbor as we love ourselves. This is called the Great Commandment. We are called to care about others. We show our love for God when we help those who are in need.

Keeping the Great Commandment

Christians are called to live by Jesus' Great Commandment of love. Some Christians care for people in their parishes. Some Christians help people who are alone. And some care for those who live right in their own neighborhoods.

This is a story about a Christian who lives out the Great Commandment.

James is a fifteen-year-old high-school freshman who lives in the busy city of Detroit. Besides his love for sports and music, James loves to read. Most of all, James loves people and enjoys being with others.

Mrs. Tompkins, who is elderly now, lives three houses down from James' family. Mrs. Tompkins is almost blind and has difficulty walking. She spends most of her time indoors, listening to the radio or TV.

James remembers when Mrs. Tompkins would sit on her front steps and read to him and the other neighborhood children. She always read wonderful, exciting stories, full of adventure and interesting characters. Story time with Mrs. Tompkins was always a special time for James.

Now James visits Mrs. Tompkins and reads to her. James brings books of poetry, short stories, and sometimes a long novel. The two neighbors continue to do what they have always enjoyed doing—reading a good story and just spending time together.

Activity

Complete the following stories in a way that shows you understand the meaning of the Great Commandment.

1. Maria loved to go to Girl Scouts each Wednesday after school. One Tuesday evening Maria's mother told her she could not get a babysitter on Wednesday for Maria's little brother. Maria's mother asked Maria to give up Girl Scouts for one week and baby-sit for her little brother. Maria was very upset.

   _____

   _____

   _____

2. Paul and his friend were in the middle of playing a video game. Paul's little sister was invited to go to a friend's house to play, but she was not allowed to walk there by herself. She pleaded with Paul to walk with her to her friend's house.

   _____

   _____

   _____

3. Tom and Lisa were playing in the yard. They were having a great time until their next-door neighbor came over. He was locked out of his house. He asked them to help him find the house key that he had lost in the grass.

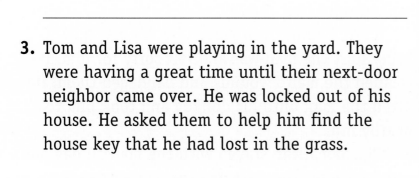

   _____

   _____

   _____

The Good Samaritan

One day a young man saw Jesus and asked him a question. "Teacher," the man asked, "what do I have to do to live always in God's love?"

Jesus answered by saying, "What do you read in Scripture?"

"You will love the Lord, your God, with all your heart, with all your soul, with all your strength, and with all your mind; and you will love your neighbor as you love yourself," the young man answered.

"That's right," Jesus said. "Do that and you will live in God's love."

The young man realized that he had just answered his own question! So the young man asked another question, "Who is my neighbor?" Then Jesus told this story.

"One day a man was going on a trip from Jerusalem to Jericho. Robbers attacked him and stole his money. They left him almost dead.

"A little later a leader of the people walked by. He saw the man lying on the side of the road. But the leader just kept walking.

"Soon a man who worked in the **Temple** came down the road. He also saw the bleeding man but walked right past him.

"Then a **Samaritan** passed by. He saw how badly hurt the man was and felt sorry for him. He cleaned the man's wounds and bandaged them. He lifted the man onto his donkey and took him to a nearby inn.

"The Samaritan stayed with the man all day and cared for him. The next day the Samaritan gave money to the owner of the inn. 'Look after this man until I come back,' he said, 'If you need to spend more money, I'll pay you when I return.'"

When the story was finished, Jesus looked at the young man and asked him, "Which of these three people acted like a neighbor to the man who was robbed?"

"The one who was kind to him," the young man answered.

Jesus said to him, "Then go and do the same."

Based on Luke 10:25–37

Activity

In the spaces below, list four words that could be used to complete the sentence.
A Good Samaritan is someone who

1. _____

2. _____

3. _____

4. _____

Vocabulary

Temple: the sacred house of worship for the Jewish people, which is located in Jerusalem

Samaritan: someone from Samaria, the land north of Jerusalem

The Stranger on the Way

David, Andy, and Jerry were on their way to soccer practice. As they neared the playing field, they noticed someone crouched on the ground, holding his legs up to his chest. Quickly the boys hurried over to see who it was. Although the boy was a stranger to the three friends, it was easy to see what had happened. A brand new bike was on the ground and both of the stranger's knees were torn out of his jeans. And from the spots of blood on the ground, one could see that his knees were probably in worse shape than his jeans.

The three friends soon discovered that the stranger's name was Tony and that Tony and his family had just moved into town three weeks before. No wonder the boys hadn't recognized him.

Tony's knees were cut and bleeding, and the palms of his hands were badly scraped. Tony was in a lot of pain, and there were tears in his eyes.

"What should we do?" Andy asked his friends.

"We can't do anything," Jerry answered, "or we'll be late for soccer practice."

David nodded in agreement and added, "Besides, what could we do anyway? We better get going."

Andy thought for a moment and then spoke up. "You guys go ahead. Tell the coach that I'll get there as soon as I can. I'm going to help Tony get home."

Jerry and David shook their heads and then ran off in the direction of the soccer field.

As he watched his friends running off, Andy helped Tony to his feet. Then, with Tony leaning on Andy, and Andy walking Tony's bike, the two boys began the long slow walk to Tony's house.

Activity

Decide how you as a fourth grader could be a neighbor to these people in need.

1. There is an elderly man who lives on your street who seems to dislike children. Every time you and your friends walk past his house, he glares at you.

2. Your school bus driver is a young mother who must bring her toddler on the bus with her every morning and afternoon. Sometimes the little girl is cranky and wants her mother's attention. Mrs. Davis tries to quiet her daughter and drive the school bus. Mrs. Davis seems to be very upset.

Praying Prayers of Petition

One kind of prayer that seems to come naturally to almost everyone is the prayer of petition. To *petition* means to ask or request. When we pray a prayer of petition, we ask God to give us what we need or to give to others what they need.

Young children first learn to pray by praying simple prayers of petition, such as "God, please make Grandma better," or "God, please give Daddy a new job."

We pray prayers of petition at Mass, too. The Prayer of the Faithful, or General Intercessions, is a prayer of petition in which we pray together for the world, our country, our Church leaders, and for those who are sick or in need.

What prayers of petition would you pray today? Write your petitions on the lines below. Then pray your prayers silently or aloud with your class.

For _____,
Lord, hear my prayer.
For _____,
Lord, hear my prayer.
For _____,
Lord, hear my prayer.

Chapter Review

Complete the sentences below with the correct words from the word box. You may use some words more than once.

ourselves	all else	Samaritan	commandment
love	neighbor	God	Great Commandment

1. Jesus teaches us to love _____ above _____ .

2. We show our love for God by our _____ for others.

3. The _____ teaches us to love our _____ as we love _____ .

4. In the Scripture story the person who stopped and helped the man who was robbed was a _____ .

5. A law given to us by God to help us live good lives by being loving people is a _____ .

Write the answers to the first two questions.

1. What does Jesus mean by the term *neighbor*?

   _____

2. What does Jesus' Great Commandment teach us?

   _____

   _____

   _____

   _____

3. Discuss what you can do to care for your neighbors.

All God's commandments may be summed up in this: You will love your neighbor as you love yourself.

Based on Romans 13:9

6

Happy Are Those...

Activity

Complete the survey by placing a ✔ in the column that best describes your level of happiness in each situation.

	JUST OKAY	HAPPY	VERY HAPPY
Winning a game			
Receiving a gift			
Getting good grades in school			
Doing a favor for someone			
Giving someone a gift			
Being with friends			
Doing something nice for my family			
Getting new clothes or new toys			

What does the word *happiness* mean to you?

True Happiness

One day, crowds of people gathered to see Jesus. Near the top of a mountain, Jesus sat down and began to teach them how to find everlasting happiness.

"Happy are the poor in spirit. The **reign of God** is theirs.

"Happy, too, are the sorrowing. They will be comforted.

"Happy are the gentle. They will receive all that God has promised.

"Happy are those who hunger and thirst for **justice**. They will be satisfied."

Jesus stopped speaking. He had more to tell the people about finding everlasting happiness and the **kingdom of heaven** but he wanted to let the people think about what he had taught them.

Based on Matthew 5:1–6

Vocabulary

reign of God: the time when God's peace, love, and justice will begin to rule our lives in this world and be fulfilled when Christ comes again

justice: loving God and all people by treating everyone fairly

kingdom of heaven: another name for the reign of God

/////////////////

Activity

List three wishes that if granted, you think would make you happy.

1. I wish _____

2. I wish _____

3. I wish _____

Lasting Happiness

Jesus was a happy man, and he taught his friends the way to everlasting happiness. The **Beatitudes** summarize how Jesus lived and how he calls us to live if we are to be truly happy in this world and the next.

Jesus promises that if we live the Beatitudes God's powerful love will change our hearts and our world. We will begin to see God's reign ruling our lives in this world. Yet the promises of the Beatitudes will only be fulfilled when Christ comes again.

1. People who are *poor in spirit* know they need God. When we are poor in spirit, we trust in God's care for us, and are thankful for the good things we have been given.

2. People who are *sorrowing* are saddened by sin and evil. When we are sorrowing, we try hard to do what is good and to change what brings suffering to others.

3. People who are *gentle* believe love is the best way to overcome evil and heal what hurts others. When we are gentle, we treat ourselves and others kindly.

4. People who *hunger and thirst for justice* want everyone to be treated fairly and equally. When we hunger and thirst for justice, we share what we have and respect all people.

Activity

Choose one of the four beatitudes listed above and circle its number. Then on the lines below, write the name of someone you know who lives that beatitude. Finally, tell what he or she does to carry out that beatitude.

_____

_____

_____

_____

_____

_____

Vocabulary

Beatitudes: the teachings of Jesus on how to gain everlasting happiness; how Jesus lived

We Believe

The eight Beatitudes are Jesus' sayings that teach us to love God and others, and promise us a place in the kingdom of heaven. Christians believe that they will be happy forever if they live Jesus' Beatitudes.

As followers of Jesus, the early Christians tried to live the Beatitudes. The Acts of the Apostles tells us how they lived.

The First Christians

The first Christians treated one another like members of a family. They lived together and shared everything. They sold their possessions and gave the money to those who were in need. They ate their meals together. They prayed together and they broke bread together in memory of Jesus.

Based on Acts 2:42–47

Signs of Justice

The first Christians were concerned for one another. Their care for the poor, the sick, and the elderly, and their equal treatment of one another, were all signs that Jesus' Beatitudes were being lived out in their lives.

The Beatitudes remind us that today's followers of Jesus must also work for justice. People who work for justice share what they have with those who are in need. People of justice respect all human beings regardless of their race, color, language, or religion.

Activity

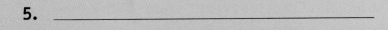

Listed below are actions that you can take to work for justice in your community. Add two more actions to the list. Then circle the action that you think is the most important.

1. I will treat all people fairly, even if they are younger than me.

2. I will believe that others are as good as I am, even if they look different.

3. I will respect those who speak a different language.

4. _____

_____

5. _____

_____

Saint Frances of Rome

Frances, born in 1384, grew up to have had everything she wanted. Her husband, Lorenzo, loved her, and she loved him. They had three beautiful children. The family was rich, and Frances had many fine things.

She prayed every day, thanking God for so many gifts. But she felt sad for people who did not have all the good things she had. So she sold her fine clothes and used the money to buy food and medicine for the poor. She even turned part of her home into a hospital.

Then there was a war. Enemies sent Frances' husband into exile and ruined their home. One son was taken prisoner. Frances' daughter and her other son died. Frances was now poor herself, but she continued to trust in God's care.

Placing her life in God's hands, Frances prayed and worked even harder for those who were sick or poor. She set up a soup kitchen and begged for food to feed the hungry.

At the end of the war, Frances' husband and son were able to return home. For the next twenty years, Frances cared for her family and continued her work for the poor and the sick. She organized a community of women to help the people of Rome.

Then Frances' husband died. Frances missed him very much. She spent even more time praying and working with her community of women to help the poor of Rome.

Frances died in 1440, four years after her husband died. The people of Rome loved her so much that they named the church where she was buried the Church of Saint Frances of Rome. Catholics celebrate the feast of Saint Frances on March 9.

Activity

Complete the Venn diagram by naming ways in which Saint Frances helped others find happiness and ways in which you help others find happiness. Are any ways the same? Write those ways in the overlapping part of the circle.

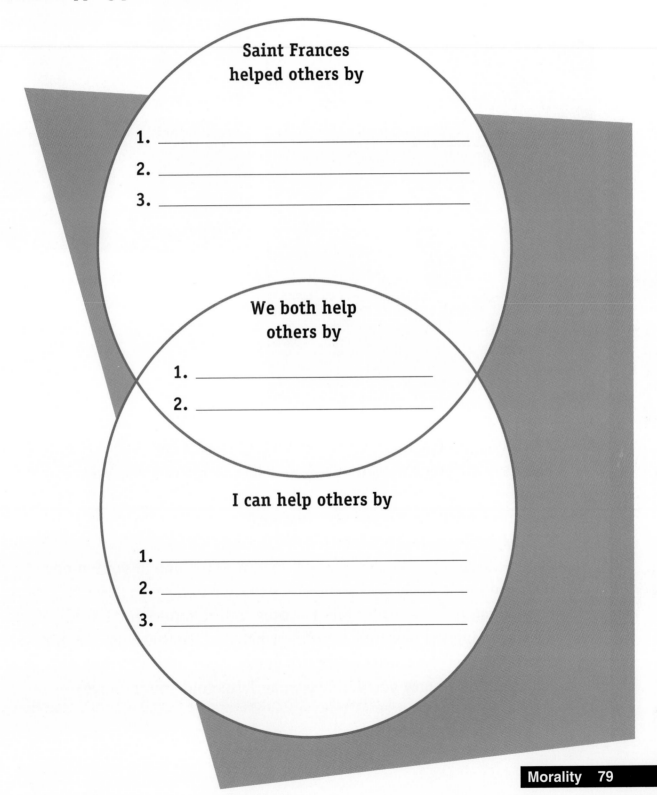

Saint Frances helped others by

1. _____

2. _____

3. _____

We both help others by

1. _____

2. _____

I can help others by

1. _____

2. _____

3. _____

Praying and Meditating

Meditation is a special kind of prayer. When we meditate, we turn all of our attention to God. We think about God. We wonder about God. We imagine ourselves in the presence of God.

There are different ways to meditate. Here is one of those ways.

1. *Prepare*: Find a quiet place. Sit comfortably. Breathe slowly and deeply until you feel peaceful.
2. *Picture*: Read a gospel story slowly. Picture the scene in your mind. Hear the words of Jesus. Imagine how it feels to be with Jesus.
3. *Pray*: When you are ready, talk to Jesus. Tell him how you feel about his words and his presence. Tell him what you are thinking. Ask him questions. Listen as Jesus speaks to you.
4. *Practice*: Decide how you will live what Jesus told you in prayer.

Chapter Review

Think of one way you and others can live each of the first four beatitudes. Write your answers on the lines provided.

1. Happy are the poor in spirit. _____

_____

_____

2. Happy are the sorrowing. _____

_____

_____

3. Happy are the gentle. _____

_____

_____

4. Happy are those who hunger and thirst

for justice.

_____

_____

Write the answers to the first two questions.

1. What are the Beatitudes?

_____

_____

2. How does Jesus say we can be happy?

_____

_____

_____

3. Discuss what we can do to bring more justice into the world.

Those who are kind to the poor will be happy.
Based on Proverbs 14:21

7

...The Reign of God Is Theirs

What are some things that help you and your classmates live peacefully and happily together instead of fighting and hurting one another?

Activity

Fill in the blanks to complete the sentences below, using your own words.

1. When I hear the word *peace*, I think of

_____ .

2. The opposite of peace is _____ .

3. A peacemaker is someone who _____ .

4. The most peaceful person I know is

_____

because _____ .

Words of Peace and Happiness

Jesus had been telling his **disciples** and many other people how to live happy lives. He had already shared with them four ways to find everlasting happiness. Now Jesus wanted to teach them more. So he began to speak again.

"Happy also are those who show **mercy** to others. They will receive mercy.

Happy are the single-hearted. They will see God.

Happy are the **peacemakers**. They will be called children of God.

Happy are those who are treated unfairly for doing what is right. The reign of God is theirs."

Jesus looked around. He could see that the people were trying to understand what he had said.

Based on Matthew 5:7–10

Vocabulary

disciples: followers of Jesus

mercy: loving care, or compassion

peacemakers: people who try to bring peace and friendship where these things are needed

//////////////////////

Activity

World leaders are often peacemakers. What advice would you give the President of the United States that might help him bring peace to the world?

_____

_____

_____

_____

_____

Ways to Everlasting Happiness

The word *beatitude* means "blessed" or "happy." The Beatitudes show us Jesus' way to eternal happiness. They let us see how Jesus lived and how he wants us to choose to live. If we live the Beatitudes, Jesus promises that we will be happy forever in the kingdom of heaven.

We learned about the first four beatitudes in Chapter 6. Now we will learn about the last four. In these four beatitudes, Jesus invites us to live as people of peace.

5. People who *show mercy* care for people who are hurting and forgive those who hurt them. When we try to understand how others feel, accept their faults, forgive them, and ease their pain, we show mercy.

6. People who are *single-hearted* keep God and his way of love first in their hearts. When what God wants us to do is more important to us than what anyone tempts us to do, we are single-hearted.

7. People who are *peacemakers* try to bring peace where there is none. When we help others stop fighting and find ways to solve problems, we are peacemakers.

8. People who are *treated unfairly* do what God wants, even when others threaten to hurt them. When we do what is right and others laugh and make fun of us, or exclude us, we are treated unfairly.

Activity

The words below describe some of the qualities found in the Beatitudes. The sentences are examples of those qualities. Match the word to the sentence by writing the correct numbers on the lines below.

1. peacefulness   _____ I believe in you.

2. understanding   _____ I'm happy when we get along.

3. mercy   _____ I know how you feel.

4. care   _____ It's okay. I forgive you.

5. trust   _____ I won't punish you unjustly.

6. forgiveness   _____ I'd like to help you.

We Believe

Jesus wants us to follow his example and his teachings so that we will be happy in this world and the next. The Beatitudes summarize Jesus' way to happiness, a way of loving and caring.

Person of the Week

TV anchor: Now our *Person of the Week*. In her troubled East Side neighborhood, this young girl took a risk that paid off. She called it *Project Peace*. Her name is Olga Frascati. Here is what she did.

Boy: There were fights all the time. I was afraid to walk down the street.

Girl: I was looking forward to moving and getting out of here. Kids sold drugs everywhere.

TV anchor: Olga decided to do something about this sad situation. With the help of people in the community, she began *Project Peace*. Olga, what is *Project Peace*?

Olga: *Project Peace* brings people together to talk about problems instead of fighting over them. We also plan fun ways for kids from different backgrounds to get to know and understand one another. We made up posters and slogans, such as "Open Your Hands to Help, Not Hurt." A group of kids wrote and recorded a great rap song, which they call "Melting Down Hearts."

TV anchor: Mr. Harrison, the East Side councilman, supports Olga. Mr. Harrison, what is Olga accomplishing?

Mr. Harrison: Olga is making a great difference. *Project Peace* has reduced violence in this neighborhood. Everyone is much happier. People are starting to respect each other. There's even a growing neighborhood spirit. She's a brave young girl.

TV anchor: For those reasons, we at WXYZ-TV are proud to honor Olga Frascati as our *Person of the Week*.

Signs of Peace

As followers of Jesus, the early Christians tried to live the Beatitudes. The Bible tells us what the disciples taught others about peace.

Turn from wrong ways. Along with all those who call Jesus the Lord, seek faith, and love, and peace. Do not cause quarrels, because the follower of the Lord must not be quarrelsome. Rather, you must be kind to all.

Based on 2 Timothy 2:22–24

Hebrew and Aramaic were the languages of Jesus' people. In Hebrew, the word **shalom** means many things. Shalom means freedom from violence or misfortune. Shalom also means **wholeness**, well-being, and peace. When we work for peace, we work for much more than freedom from violence. We also work for the well-being of all people, and for wholeness for ourselves and others. The Beatitudes call us to work for shalom.

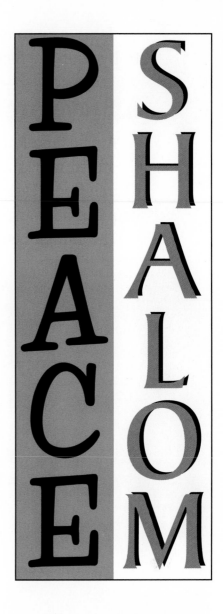

Vocabulary

shalom: the Hebrew word for peace, wholeness, well-being, and freedom from violence

wholeness: being a complete person; having peace, faith, acceptance, and wellness

Jesus' way to eternal happiness is not always easy. It takes courage to live out the Beatitudes. Archbishop Oscar Romero had such courage.

A Brave Archbishop

Archbishop Romero stood silently in a small church in El Salvador. He stared with shock at the body of the parish priest lying on the church floor. Father Rutilio Grande had been killed because he lived to help the poor and worked for justice and peace.

The church began to fill up with people. They wept for their priest.

They prayed for those who had killed their pastor and sang hymns of hope.

The archbishop prayed, too. "What can I do," he thought, "to bring peace and justice to my country?"

At that time, many people who tried to help the poor were put in jail, were tortured, and were killed. Many were never seen again.

"Jesus was always with the poor," Archbishop Romero thought to himself. "The Church needs to be with the poor, too. I must do all I can to help my people and to stop the killing."

Archbishop Romero began to speak out for the rights of the poor. He knew how they were hurting. His words, echoing their pain, gave hope to the poor as they listened to his radio talks each week.

Archbishop Romero received many death threats, but he continued to speak out for justice and peace. He begged those who were killing to put down their guns. He offered mercy and forgiveness to those who did so.

On March 24, 1980, as Archbishop Romero was celebrating the Eucharist, two men shot him through the heart and killed him.

Many people in El Salvador and around the world honor Archbishop Oscar Romero as a martyr.

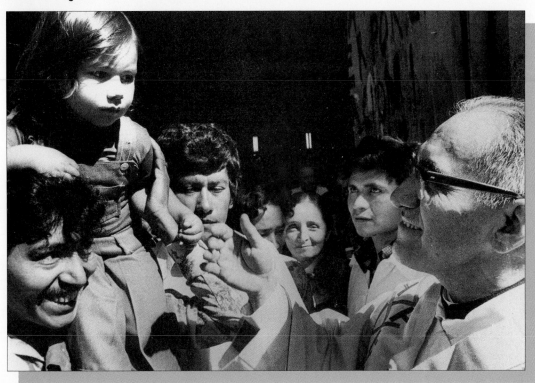

Activity

Put a ✓ in front of the words you think Archbishop Romero might have preached.

1. _____ "You shall love one another."

2. _____ "Be peacemakers."

3. _____ "Fight, fight, fight."

4. _____ "Do not hurt the poor."

5. _____ "God loves you very much."

6. _____ "If people hurt you, hurt them back."

7. _____ "Be a disciple of Jesus. Care for the poor."

8. _____ "Forget about the suffering."

9. _____ "Treat others the way you would have them treat you."

10. _____ "Forgive those who hurt you."

Praying the Jesus Prayer

The Jesus Prayer is a simple prayer that can bring peace to our minds and hearts. By prayerfully repeating the name of Jesus, we can begin to feel the peace that Jesus offers us. We can also pray a longer version of the Jesus Prayer: *Jesus, Son of God, have mercy on me.*

One important part of praying the Jesus Prayer is to pay attention to our breathing. As we pray *Jesus, Son of God,* we take a slow, deep breath. We breathe in the love and peace of Jesus. Then as we finish the prayer with the words *have mercy on me,* we breathe out slowly. We breathe out our worries and problems.

Spend some quiet time today praying the Jesus Prayer.

Chapter Review

Think of one way you can live each of the last four beatitudes. Write your answers on the lines after each beatitude.

Happy are those who show mercy.

_____

_____

Happy are the single-hearted.

_____

_____

Happy are the peacemakers.

_____

_____

Happy are those who are unjustly treated for doing what is right.

_____

_____

Write your answers to the first two questions on the lines provided.

1. What is meant by *disciples*?

_____

2. What does Jesus teach us in the last four beatitudes?

_____

_____

_____

_____

Jesus says, "Treat others the way you would have them treat you."
Based on Matthew 7:12

3. Discuss how you can be a peacemaker.

God's Commandments

A Computer Game

"What are you doing on the computer?" Jim asked Stephanie.

"I'm trying to play a new game," Stephanie answered. "Do you want to play?"

"Okay. Is it like a trivia game?" Jim asked.

"No," said Stephanie. "It's about rules, all kinds of rules. Here's how it works."

"Six boys and girls get into a spaceship. They blast off and go through space for a few days. Then the boys and girls see a planet that looks like Earth, but it's much smaller. They get closer to the planet. They can see water, plants, and even animals on the planet. But there are no people. They land their spaceship."

"Sounds like fun!" Jim said. "How do you play?"

"We decide which rules the boys and girls will need to live on the planet," Stephanie explained. "The winner of the game is the player who chooses the most important rules."

What are some rules and laws that are part of your daily life? Why are laws and rules important?

Rules to Live By

We can read in the Bible about the special rules that God has given to us. These rules are called the **Ten Commandments.** The Ten Commandments are rules that God has given us to help us live good lives.

Jesus taught the Great Commandment of love and the Beatitudes. They show us how to live like Jesus. But Jesus says that keeping the Ten Commandments is also important. If we do all these things, we can follow Jesus and live as he lived.

The Ten Commandments

1. I, the Lord, am your God. You shall not have other gods besides me.

2. You shall not take the name of the Lord, your God, in vain.

3. Remember to keep holy the Sabbath.

4. Honor your father and your mother.

5. You shall not kill.

6. You shall not commit adultery.

7. You shall not steal.

8. You shall not bear false witness against your neighbor.

9. You shall not covet your neighbor's wife.

10. You shall not covet anything that belongs to your neighbor.

Based on Exodus 20:2–17 and Deuteronomy 5:6–21

Vocabulary

Ten Commandments: the ten special rules given to us by God to help us live good lives

/////////////////

We Believe

The Church teaches that the Ten Commandments are God's laws. They are ways of showing love for God and for other people. The Ten Commandments are laws that help us live together in peace and happiness.

The Rich Young Man ~~~~~

One day, Jesus was walking from one town to another. Along the way a rich young man ran up to him. He bowed to Jesus and asked him a question.

"Good Teacher, what must I do to live always in God's love?"

Reminding the man of God's laws, Jesus answered, "You know the commandments:
    You shall not kill;
    You shall not commit adultery;
    You shall not steal;
    You shall not cheat;
Honor your father and your mother.'"

The young man smiled happily. "But, Teacher," he said to Jesus, "I have kept all these laws since I was a child."

Jesus looked at the man and smiled. "There is one more thing you should do," Jesus told him. "Go and sell what you have and give to the poor; then you will be rich in **heaven**. After that, come and follow me."

The smile left the man's face as he listened to Jesus speak. Sadness filled the man's eyes. He did not want to give his money away. He turned around and sadly walked away, for he was very rich.

Based on Mark 10:17–22

Beyond the Law

Jesus reminded the young man in the Scripture story of God's commandments. Jesus told him then and tells us today that keeping the Ten Commandments is an important part of being disciples and necessary for being truly happy. The Ten Commandments are ways of showing love for God and for other people. The commandments are laws that help us live together in peace and happiness.

But Jesus didn't stop there. He taught that there is more to being one of his friends and followers than keeping the Ten Commandments. Jesus' Great Commandment and the Beatitudes ask us to go beyond simple obedience to God's laws.

Activity

On the lines below, name an action that goes beyond the law. The first one is done for you.

1. **Law:** Do not steal.

   Beyond the law: Always ask your brother's or sister's permission before borrowing his or her possessions.

2. **Law:** Tell the truth.

   Beyond the law: _____

   _____

3. **Law:** Don't be mean to others.

   Beyond the law: _____

Vocabulary

heaven: being with God forever

//////////////////////

Activity

Name one rule that makes each of the communities listed below work better. Then explain why each rule works.

PLACE	RULE	WHY RULE WORKS
HOME		
SCHOOL		
CLUB OR TEAM		

Toward Justice and Peace

The New Testament gives us many examples of how important the commandments of God are to every Christian. Here is one example taken from the Second Letter of John.

I make this request of you, although it is a commandment we have had from the start: Let us love one another.

To love one another means that we must live according to the commandments.

Based on 2 John 5–6

The Ten Commandments guide us in living our lives as people of peace and justice. We can bring peace and justice into our families and classroom by the way we show our love for God and for one another.

We work for peace and justice each time we play a game fairly, allowing everyone to have his or her turn.

We work for peace and justice each time we stand up for someone who is falsely accused or treated unkindly, even if our friends don't support us.

We work for peace and justice each time we pray for people around our country and around our world who don't have enough to eat because others have too much.

We show our love for God by keeping the commandments. The first three commandments teach us how to love and serve God. The remaining seven commandments teach us how to love and serve one another.

Activity

Put a ✓ in front of the sentences below that tell how you can bring peace and justice to your family and classroom.

_____ **1.** I can try not to argue with my brothers and sisters.

_____ **2.** I can play fairly on the playground.

_____ **3.** I can do my chores without reminders.

_____ **4.** I can cooperate with my teachers and principal.

_____ **5.** I can obey school rules.

What Do the Commandments Mean?

The laws of God that we know as the Ten Commandments are meant to help people of all ages live lives of justice and peace. Here are some ways in which fourth graders can live God's laws.

First Commandment
I remember to pray.
Second Commandment
I speak God's name only in prayer or in conversation about God.
Third Commandment
I attend Mass each Sunday.
Fourth Commandment
I respect and obey my parents.
Fifth Commandment
I am careful not to say mean or hurtful things to others.

Sixth Commandment
I respect my body and the bodies of others.
Seventh Commandment
I treat other people's property with care.
Eighth Commandment
I always try to tell the whole truth.
Ninth Commandment
I respect the promises that married people have made to each other.
Tenth Commandment
I try not to be greedy or jealous.

Activity

You are the editor of your school newspaper. You have just received two Letters to the Editor. Write a short response to each letter.

Page 4

Angel Press

School Newspaper of Saint Michael the Archangel Elementary School

Dear Editor,

Recently a girl from your school came to deliver cookies that your school is selling. When I paid for the cookies, I gave her too much money. She quickly showed me my mistake and made sure that she was paid only the correct amount.

We are lucky to have such an honest girl in our neighborhood. And Saint Michael's should feel proud to have such an honest student in its fourth-grade class.

Sincerely,
Mr. Roger Brown

_____

_____

_____

_____

_____

_____

_____

_____

_____

Dear Editor,

The other day I left my new jacket out on the playground when I went into school. Luckily for me, the person who found it brought the jacket to the principal's office and I got it back.

I would just like to thank the person who returned my jacket.

Sincerely,
Amy Anderson
Grade 4

_____

_____

_____

_____

_____

_____

_____

_____

_____

Praying for Peace and Justice

Leader: Today we bring our desire for true peace and justice before the Lord. We ask the Lord to create new hearts in us so that we may not only *pray* for peace and justice but rather, that we may *live* for peace and justice.

Reader: Let us listen carefully to a reading from the Gospel of Mark.
(Read Mark 10:17-22.)

All: Praise to you, Lord Jesus Christ.

Leader: Let us turn our thoughts to thoughts of peace by praying together the following prayer of Saint Francis of Assisi.

All: Lord, make me an instrument of
your peace.
Where there is hatred, let me sow love;
where there is injury, pardon;
where there is doubt, faith;
where there is despair, hope;
where there is darkness, light.
O divine master, grant that I may not
so much seek to be consoled
as to console;
to be understood as to understand;
to be loved as to love;
for it is in giving that we receive;
it is in pardoning that we
are pardoned;
and it is in dying that we are born to
eternal life.

Leader: Let us end our prayer as people of peace and justice.

All: Amen.

Chapter Review

Read these news headlines. Beside each one, write the name of a commandment the headline relates to.

Police Make Arrest in Murder Case

Police Investigate Credit Card Cheats

President Attends Church in Tennessee

Teenager Admits Selling Drugs in School Hallway

Union Leader Accused of Lying About Mob

Child Injured in Fall; Ignored Mother's Warnings

Wife of Attorney Says Husband Was Unfaithful

Department Store Prices Up Due to Rise in Thefts

Write the answers to the first two questions.

1. What is meant by *heaven*?

_____

_____

2. What do the Ten Commandments help us to do?

_____

_____

_____

_____

3. Discuss what you can do to be a better disciple of Jesus.

> Those who live by the Lord's commandments will be happy.
> **Based on Psalm 119:1–2**

UNIT ORGANIZER

----FOLLOWING THE WAY OF LOVE----

List the most important ideas you've learned about in each chapter listed below.

Chapter 5
The Great Commandment

Chapter 6
Happy Are Those...

Chapter 8
God's Commandments

Chapter 7
...The Reign of God Is Theirs

UNIT 2 REVIEW

Circle the word(s) to complete each sentence.

1. Jesus taught the Beatitudes to show us how to be _____ .
   rich   selfish   happy

2. Jesus wants us to act as he did and _____ people who have hurt us.
   ignore   forgive   fight with

3. God's love will bring freedom, justice, and peace to _____ .

   only the single-hearted   only the merciful   everyone

4. _____ worked for justice and peace in El Salvador.

   Francis of Assisi   Archbishop Romero   Martin de Porres

Match the first part of each commandment in Column A with its second part in Column B.

Column A

1. I, the Lord, am your God. You shall not have

2. You shall not take the name of

3. Remember to keep holy

4. Honor

5. You shall not

6. You shall not commit

7. You shall not

8. You shall not bear false witness against

9. You shall not covet

10. You shall not covet

Column B

_____ adultery.

_____ anything that belongs to your neighbor.

_____ your neighbor.

_____ steal.

_____ other gods besides me.

_____ your father and your mother.

_____ the Lord, your God, in vain.

_____ the Sabbath.

_____ kill.

_____ your neighbor's wife.

UNIT 2 REVIEW

Write **True** if the sentence is true, and **False** is the sentence is false.

1. _____ A neighbor is just the person who lives next door.

2. _____ The reign of God will be present in its fullness when Christ comes again.

3. _____ Justice means loving all our neighbors and treating everyone fairly.

4. _____ A beatitude is one of the signs of the Holy Spirit.

5. _____ The disciples were friends and followers of the Good Samaritan.

6. _____ Peacemakers are those who try to bring peace and friendship only in times of war.

Fill in the missing word(s) to complete each sentence.

1. Jesus' teaching to love God above all things and to love our neighbor as we love ourselves is called the _____.

2. The _____ are people who know they need God.

3. We are called to care about others as the _____ did.

4. The Ten Commandments are God's _____.

5. The _____ will be with God forever.

6. _____ is being with God and those he loves forever.

7. The Ten Commandments are ways of showing love for _____ and for _____.

DECIDING WHAT'S RIGHT and WHAT'S WRONG

A choice between what is right and wrong is called a *moral choice*. We use our conscience to help us decide the right thing to do. Sometimes we are tempted to do things that are wrong and we know clearly that they are wrong. At other times we may be unsure about what is right and what is wrong. We call these times of uncertainty *moral dilemmas*. The following guide can be helpful at these times of uncertainty.

GUIDE for MAKING GOOD CHOICES

Step One: I can think about what I want to do and why I want to do it.

Step Two: I can think about the possible consequences of my choice.

Step Three: I can ask for advice from someone I trust.

Step Four: I can pray for guidance.

Step Five: I can ask myself if this choice shows that I am a follower of Jesus.

Help Juanita do the right thing by reading the story and answering the questions below.

Lucy is a new girl in school this year. No one really likes Lucy. She is bossy and always wants her own way. Because of how she treats others, Lucy has no friends. Juanita feels sorry for Lucy. She thinks that Lucy probably feels lonely and wants to have friends. Some of Juanita's friends are finding ways to get back at Lucy for the way she acts toward them. Juanita disagrees with how her friends are acting, but she is unsure about what to do. Juanita considers all the possible ways she could act.

- She could continue to ignore the situation and let Lucy deal with the problem.
- She could go along with her friends and begin to treat Lucy in the same way.
- She could try to help her friends and Lucy get along better.

What do you think Juanita should do?

_____

Why do you think Juanita should do this?

_____

If Juanita chooses to do this, what might be a consequence of her choice?

_____

Does this choice show Juanita to be a follower of Jesus? Why or why not?

_____

Figuring out the right thing to do isn't always easy. Sometimes it is helpful to seek advice from someone who is older and more experienced. Even though Juanita has considered her various options and their consequences, she's still uncertain about what to do. List two people Juanita might ask for advice.

_____ _____

Jesus is always available to help us when we are trying to make decisions between right and wrong actions. Through prayer we can ask Jesus for his help. Use the space below to write a prayer that Juanita might use when seeking Jesus' help.

_____

_____

_____

Following Jesus

Jesus calls us to love one another as he has loved us. When faced with difficult choices, it is important to consider whether or not our decision is a loving one. Could someone be physically hurt by what we choose to do? Could feelings be hurt? Or, do our actions spread Jesus' love by bringing peace and justice?

PRAYER

Jesus, I know you are always with me. Help me to know right from wrong. Help me to act in ways that show I am your follower. Amen.

OPENING DOORS

A Take-Home Magazine™

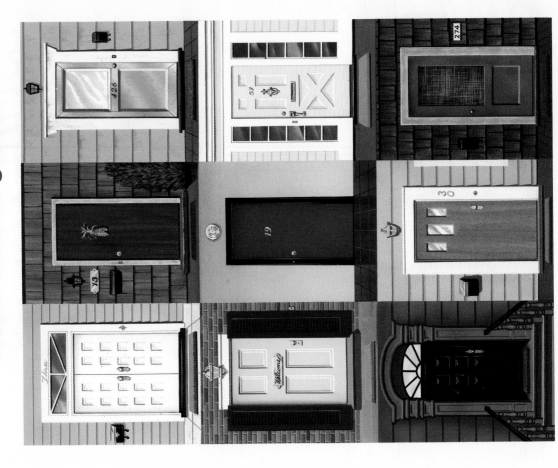

THIS IS OUR FAITH

Growing Closer

WRITE FAMILY COMMANDMENTS to nurture and remind each other about the importance of family sharing. Use the two commandments below as models for writing.

Write your list of commandments on construction paper. Display the commandments where family members will read them often. Check yourself regularly to see how you are doing at implementing them.

Do not steal precious time from being with each other; time passes too quickly to waste.

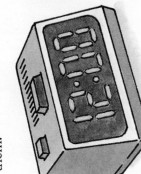

Do not wish for anyone else's life; no one else possesses the gift of each person in our family.

Looking Ahead

Unit 3 will take a closer look at the commandments that help us show respect for God, ourselves, other people, and all God's creation. Your fourth grader will learn that we are called to express love by worshiping God, honoring our parents, respecting life, and being faithful in marriage.

8

Loving Frames of Mind

One of the subtle ways you can reinforce Jesus' teaching about the Christian ways of love, justice, and peace is by sharing stories with your child. You may choose to read aloud with your child. Or, each of you may want to read separately and then discuss the story when you have the opportunity.

Happy are
the poor
in spirit…

Other Bells for Us to Ring. Robert Cormier. Dell, 1992.

Frederick. Leo Lionni. Knopf Books, 1967.

Happy are
they
who mourn…

The Big Wave. Pearl S. Buck. HarperCollins, 1986.

Saint
St. Isaac Jogues
St. Frances Xavier Cabrini
St. Rose Philippine Duchesne
St. Elizabeth Ann Seton
St. John Neumann
Bl. Katherine Drexel
Bl. Kateri Tekakwitha
Bl. Junipero Serra

Reading with Your Child

You may want to read a biography about one of the saints listed above who worked in the United States.

The Communion of Saints

Many Christians reflect Christ's presence and way of life in both ordinary and extraordinary ways. They can be models for us as we struggle to follow Jesus in our everyday lives. Some of these Christians may be in our own families, neighborhoods, or parishes.

The Church canonizes some exceptional followers of Jesus and calls them saints. All Christians, both living and dead, are part of the communion of saints. Mary, the mother of Jesus, is the greatest of all saints. The process of canonization includes the following three steps:

1. If it can be proved that a deceased Church member has led a life of extraordinary holiness and heroic virtue, then he or she is nominated to receive the title, "venerable."

2. If, after this title is conferred, a miracle is worked in this person's name, then the person receives the title "blessed." He or she is given a special feast day on the Church calendar.

3. If a second miracle is performed in this person's name, the Church declares him or her a "saint."

A Taste of Blackberries. Doris B. Smith. HarperCollins, 1988.

My Shalom, My Peace. Jacob Zim. McGraw-Hill, 1975.

Happy are the peacemakers…

The War with Grandpa. Robert Kimmel Smith. Dell, 1984.

Happy are those who hunger and thirst for justice…

Lupita Mañana. Patricia Beatty. Morrow, 1992.

Secret City, U.S.A. Felice Holman. Simon & Schuster, 1993.

You Are Invited

"Happy are those who are called to his supper." These words are spoken by the priest at Mass shortly before we receive Communion. Similar words in Scripture give us an insight into the meaning and use of the words in the Mass.

When Jesus was a dinner guest at the home of one of the Pharisees, he began telling the other guests parables. One of these parables which you can read in Luke 14:16–24 is about a man planning a great feast. The point of the parable is that the invited guests made excuses and refused to come. Therefore, the host ordered his servants to go out into the streets and alleys to bring

in the poor and the crippled, the blind and the lame, and anyone they could find who was willing to share in the feast.

It is important for us to remember that we are invited not only to share in the Eucharist but also to partake of the heavenly banquet. We have been gathered from the East and the West. We come as we are to become the people of God, to be shaped by the law and the beatitudes, to become poor in spirit, gentle, merciful, just and loving.

We come to the Eucharist in response to God's invitation. We come not only in response to the commandments to love and worship God but also to become the people who can truly love others. The Eucharist gives us the strength to obey God's law and to realize that the reign of God is within us.

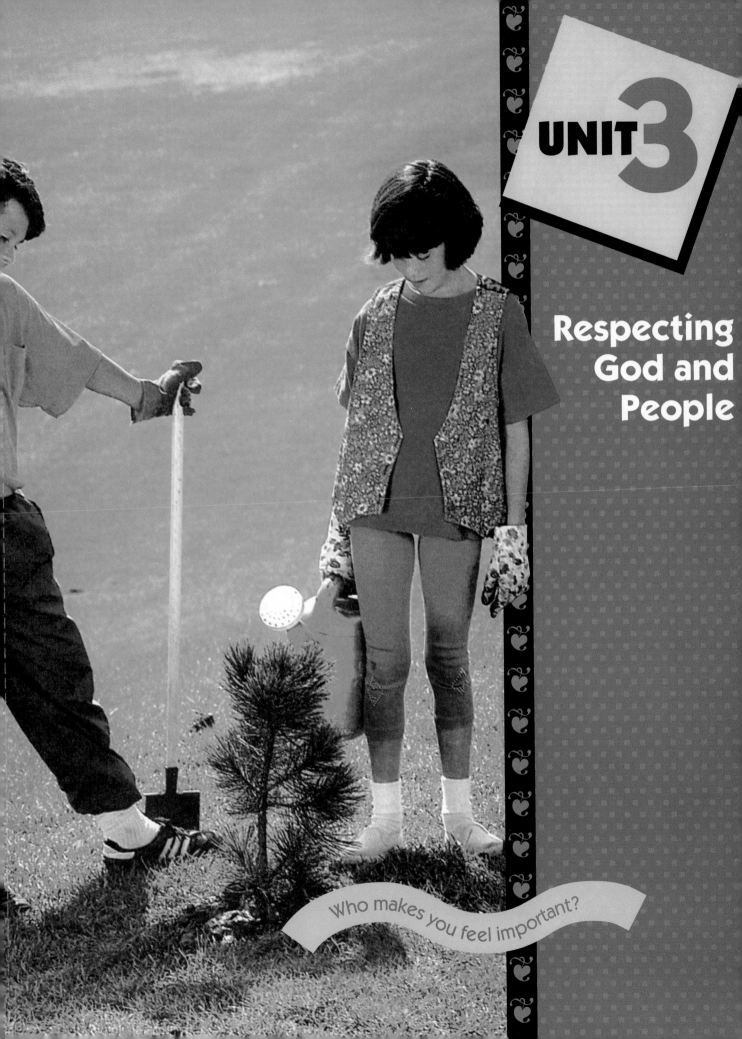

UNIT 3

Respecting God and People

Who makes you feel important?

Worshiping God

Who are some of the important people in your life? Why are these people important to you?

Activity

How can you tell that the people in the photographs are important to one another? On the lines below, write what you think they might be saying to each other.

1. _____   2. _____

_____   _____

_____   _____

_____   _____

_____   _____

Jesus Gives Us an Example

Jesus loved the good things God created. In the gospel stories, we read that Jesus enjoyed the gifts of creation. He walked by the sea. He taught on the mountainside.

Jesus taught that people are more important than things. People are the most important part of God's creation. The gospels tell us how Jesus showed his love for people. He cared for the poor. He forgave sinners. He healed the sick. He cared for and taught his disciples.

Yet there was Someone more important than people or things. God was the most important of all. Jesus' Great Commandment teaches us to love God above all else. It reminds us of the first three commandments.

Activity

Think about why God is important to you. Complete each sentence by writing your reasons on the lines.

1. God is important to me because

_____

2. God is important to me because

_____

3. God is important to me because

_____

4. God is important to me because

_____

People see certain things in their lives as more important than other things. The important things become the **values** that direct their lives and for which they live and sometimes die.

Look at the Wheel of Values below. Start with the **F** at the top of the wheel and then skip every other letter. Use the letters to write a word in the blank spaces, completing the sentences below. The sentences tell you about the selfish values some people have.

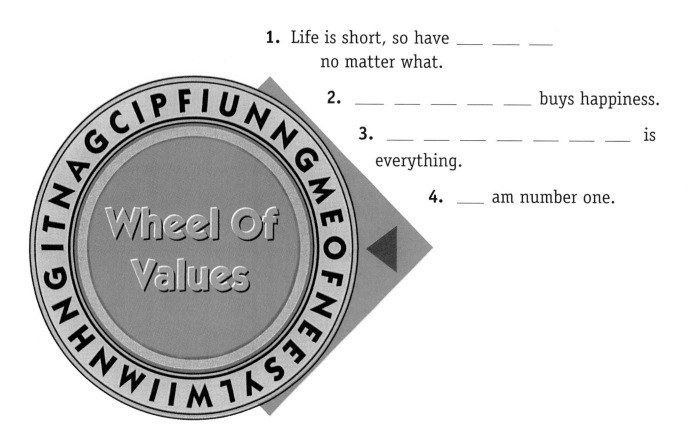

1. Life is short, so have ___ ___ ___ no matter what.

2. ___ ___ ___ ___ ___ buys happiness.

3. ___ ___ ___ ___ ___ ___ ___ is everything.

4. ___ am number one.

Understanding the Commandments

Because of God's great love for us, he gives us the Ten Commandments to live by. These laws, or rules, are given by God to help us learn the values that will guide us in living good lives.

The first three commandments teach us how to love and serve God.

1. The first commandment is *I, the Lord, am your God. You shall not have other gods besides me*. It teaches us to keep God first in our lives. No person or thing is to be more important to us than God is. No person or thing is to come between God and us. We remember God's goodness, and we talk and listen to God in prayer.

2. The second commandment is *You shall not take the name of the Lord, your God,* **in vain**. It teaches us to show respect for God. We show respect through words and actions. We use the names of God, Jesus, and all holy persons with respect and love. We treat holy places and things with reverence. We never say God's or Jesus' name without care, or use their names to express anger.

Vocabulary

values: what people consider important

in vain: in a disrespectful way

Sabbath: the weekly day of prayer and rest: Sunday for Christians, Saturday for Jews, and Friday for Muslims

We Believe

The first three commandments teach us to place God first in our lives. We learn to use God's name with respect. And we learn to honor God in a special way each Sunday.

3. The third commandment is *Remember to keep holy the* **Sabbath**. It teaches us to honor God in a special way on Sundays and holy days. Sunday is the Christian Sabbath. We worship God by celebrating the Eucharist together each Sunday. Sunday is also a day for rest and prayer. We relax and do special things on Sunday in honor of God.

Jesus teaches us that God is more important than anyone or anything in life.

Jesus Goes to the Temple

One day Jesus went to the Temple with his disciples to pray.

Jesus saw that the Temple court, or entrance, was very crowded. People were selling doves and shouting out their sale prices. Others were pushing people out of their way. Money changers sat at tables with stacks of coins, exchanging money for customers.

Jesus became very angry. He saw that the people were not putting God first even in the holy Temple. Jesus knew that people needed to exchange their money. He knew that they needed to buy doves. Jesus was not against buying or selling. But it seemed to him that business in the Temple had become more important to people than prayer.

Jesus felt that this was wrong. He turned over the tables of the money changers. Coins rolled all over the floor. Then Jesus called out to the surprised crowd. He reminded the people of God's laws, saying, "My house will be called a house of prayer for all people. But you have turned it into a den of thieves."

Based on Mark 11:15–17

Respect for God

Jesus became angry when he saw that people did not show respect for God and for God's house. As Catholics we show a special respect for God's sacred dwelling place, the church, for we know that God is present there in a special way. We also treat other holy places and things with respect and **reverence**. We try to act in ways that show that God is first in our lives.

Activity

Complete the following statements.

1. I show respect for my parish church by

_____.

2. When I receive the Eucharist, I show reverence by

_____.

3. When I am at Mass, I show respect for God by

_____.

4. I show respect for the Bible by

_____.

5. When I pray, I show respect for God by

_____.

Vocabulary

reverence: an attitude of respect and care

It is not always easy to keep God first in one's life, but the Holy Spirit and the example of others can help us. Thomas More is a good example of someone who always kept God first in his life.

Thomas More

Thomas More enjoyed life. He loved his wife and their four children. They lived in a beautiful home just outside London, England. Thomas was very happy when he was at home with his family.

Thomas liked everything in his life, but he loved God most of all. "Praise God and be merry," Thomas used to say.

Thomas was well-liked by everyone. When Henry VIII became king, he named Thomas More the Lord Chancellor of England, the second most powerful man in the country.

Then King Henry decided to make himself the head of the Church. But Thomas knew that the pope was the leader of the Church, so Thomas disapproved of what the king was doing.

This made the king very angry. The king decided to put Thomas in prison. Thomas' family begged him to honor the king as head of the Church. Thomas loved his family very much, but he knew that he could not put his love for them before his love for God.

The king then ordered that Thomas More be put to death. Before his death in 1535, Thomas said, "I die the king's good servant, but God's first." The Church honors Thomas More as a saint on June 22.

Discuss

Why did Thomas More not do what the king asked of him?

Activity

Complete each of the stories. Then write in the box the number of the commandment that matches the story.

1. The Sabbath is a special day at the Diaz house. On Sunday morning everyone gets ready to

_____ .

While they are there, they _____

_____ .

At the end of the day, they remember God's

goodness by _____

_____

_____ .

Which commandment does this story match? ☐

2. Maureen is an altar server at Saint Ann Parish. Father Charles thinks Maureen is one of the best altar servers because of the way

_____

_____ .

Some of Maureen's friends swear and curse a

lot, but Maureen says _____

_____ .

Which commandment does this story match? ☐

3. Karim's oldest brother believes that the most important thing in life is to have lots of money. Karim told him that he thinks

_____

_____ .

Which commandment does this story match? ☐

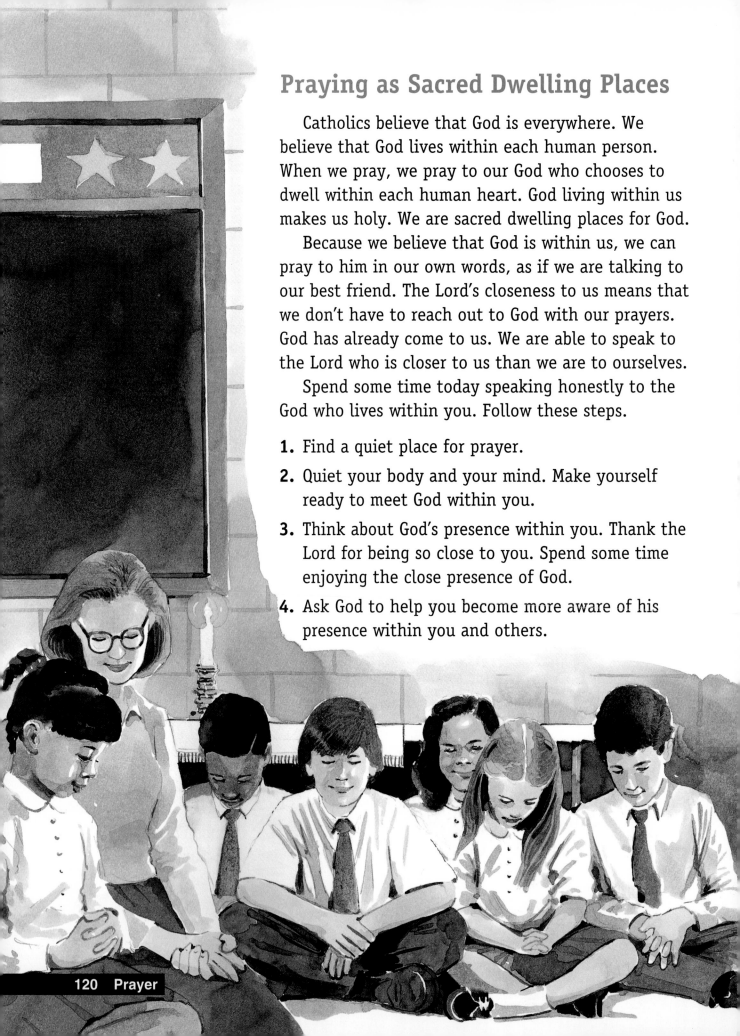

Praying as Sacred Dwelling Places

Catholics believe that God is everywhere. We believe that God lives within each human person. When we pray, we pray to our God who chooses to dwell within each human heart. God living within us makes us holy. We are sacred dwelling places for God.

Because we believe that God is within us, we can pray to him in our own words, as if we are talking to our best friend. The Lord's closeness to us means that we don't have to reach out to God with our prayers. God has already come to us. We are able to speak to the Lord who is closer to us than we are to ourselves.

Spend some time today speaking honestly to the God who lives within you. Follow these steps.

1. Find a quiet place for prayer.

2. Quiet your body and your mind. Make yourself ready to meet God within you.

3. Think about God's presence within you. Thank the Lord for being so close to you. Spend some time enjoying the close presence of God.

4. Ask God to help you become more aware of his presence within you and others.

Chapter Review

Read each statement below. Then write **True** or **False** on the line in front of each statement.

_____ 1. Jesus' Great Commandment to love God above all else reminds us of the first three commandments.

_____ 2. The money changers had great respect and reverence for God's holy Temple.

_____ 3. Thomas More disapproved of King Henry VIII's action in making himself head of the Church.

_____ 4. Thomas More was put in prison and then put to death for his beliefs.

_____ 5. Thomas More put his love of family before his love for God.

On the lines provided, write your answers to the first two questions.

1. What is meant by _in vain_?

_____

2. What do the first three commandments teach us?

_____

_____

_____

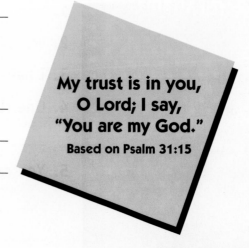

My trust is in you, O Lord; I say, "You are my God."
Based on Psalm 31:15

3. Discuss how we can place God first in our lives.

10

Honoring Our Parents

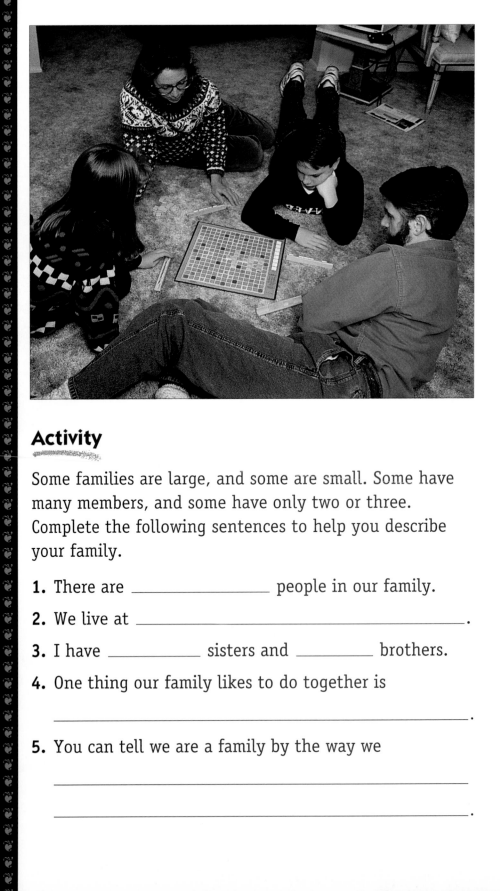

Think of how your parents show their love for you. How do you show your love for them?

Activity

Some families are large, and some are small. Some have many members, and some have only two or three. Complete the following sentences to help you describe your family.

1. There are _____ people in our family.

2. We live at _____.

3. I have _____ sisters and _____ brothers.

4. One thing our family likes to do together is

_____.

5. You can tell we are a family by the way we

_____

_____.

The Fourth Commandment

People who love and care for one another and live together make up a family. Some families have two parents and their children. Some families are made up of a mother and her children. Others have a father and his children. Sometimes families include grandparents who live with them.

Jesus wants us to respect our parents and our grandparents as Jesus respected Mary and Joseph.

The fourth commandment calls us to love our parents and to show our love in what we say and do. We are to **respect** our parents and others who are responsible for us and who care for us. We are to **obey** them unless they tell us to do something that is not good. We are also to pray for them and help them.

Throughout his life, Jesus honored his mother and his foster father. By doing this he was obeying the fourth commandment. The fourth commandment is ***Honor** your father and your mother*. When we honor our parents, we are following Jesus' example.

Vocabulary

respect: to act with care toward someone or something

obey: to do what someone who is responsible for you tells you to do

honor: to treat with respect

We Believe

The fourth commandment teaches us to love, honor, and obey our parents and others who are responsible for us.

Activity

Talk about the family in each photograph. On the lines near the photographs, tell how the people are showing respect and care for each other.

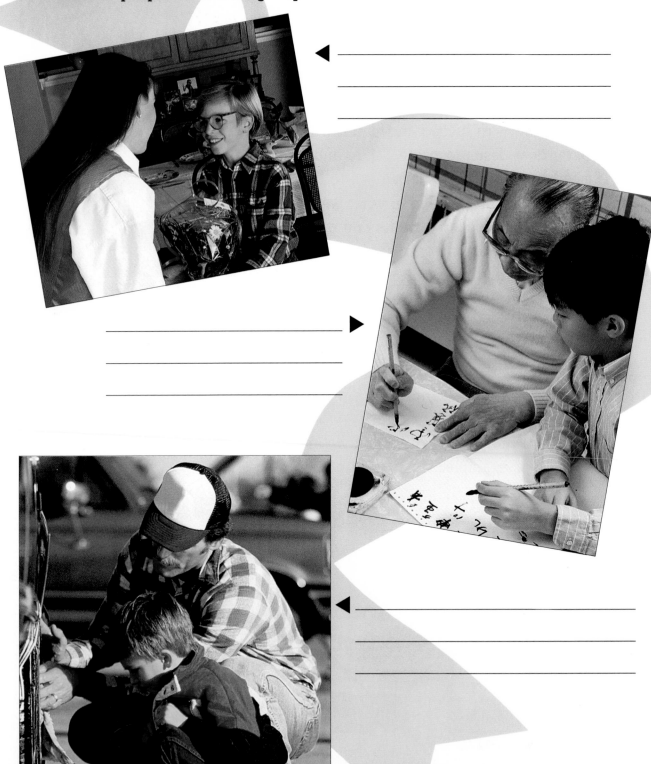

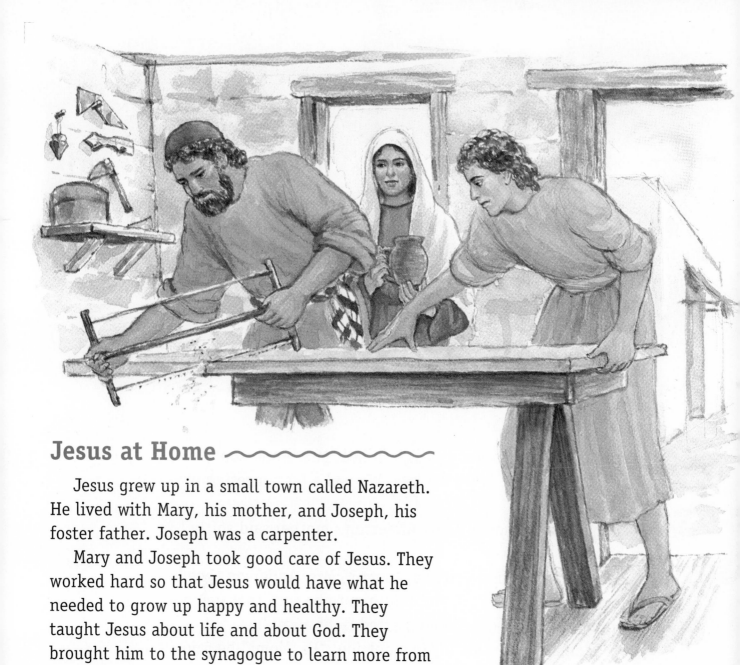

Jesus at Home

Jesus grew up in a small town called Nazareth. He lived with Mary, his mother, and Joseph, his foster father. Joseph was a carpenter.

Mary and Joseph took good care of Jesus. They worked hard so that Jesus would have what he needed to grow up happy and healthy. They taught Jesus about life and about God. They brought him to the synagogue to learn more from the rabbis.

Mary and Joseph taught Jesus to pray. The family prayed together in the morning, afternoon, and evening. They praised and thanked God at mealtimes. They celebrated the Sabbath at home and in the synagogue.

Jesus loved his parents. He obeyed them and helped them. He learned to be a carpenter in Joseph's shop. Under Mary's and Joseph's care, Jesus grew in wisdom, age, and grace.

Based on Luke 2:39–40, 51–52

Caring for Grandma

Mrs. Anderson's mother was sick in bed. Mrs. Anderson called out, "Hi, Mom! Sorry I'm late. We had a long meeting at the office."

"I'm glad you're home," Mrs. Anderson's mother said softly. "I'm hungry."

"Didn't Michael bring you your lunch?" Mrs. Anderson asked. "I called Michael from work and told him to be sure that you got something to eat. I'll get dinner started right away."

Just then Michael came in from outside. "Hi, Mom!" he said with a big smile on his face.

"Michael, Grandma is hungry and very upset. I asked you to make lunch for her. Why didn't you do it?"

"I was going to," Michael explained. "But Chrissy and Peter asked me to play ball with them. I ran out to play and forgot all about Grandma's lunch."

Then Mrs. Anderson asked Michael to sit down. "Grandma is my mother," she told him. "She took good care of me when I was growing up. Now she needs my care. I want you to be good to her, too."

"I'm sorry, Mom," Michael answered with his head down.

"You can bring Grandma her dinner in a little while," Mrs. Anderson said. "And please tell her you're sorry and you'll never forget her lunch again."

We Honor Our Parents

We do not come into the world alone. We do not grow up by ourselves. The fourth commandment reminds us that parents are a great gift to us. We show that we appreciate the gift of parents by following the fourth commandment.

We honor our parents by helping at home, by listening to their advice, and by obeying their rules. We treat them with respect in all we say and do. Even when we are grown, we continue to help them, care for them, and treat them with love and respect.

Activity

Think of what it means to honor your father and mother throughout your life. Then answer these questions.

1. How did I follow the fourth commandment when I was in first grade?

_____

2. How do I honor my father and mother now as a fourth grader?

_____

3. How might I follow the fourth commandment when I am sixteen?

_____

4. How might I follow the fourth commandment when I am my parents' age?

_____

Parents Are People, Too

Being a parent is not always easy. Parents and other adults who care for us work hard to help us. They want us to grow up to be good people. They try to make our lives safe, comfortable, and happy. Sometimes they feel worried, angry, or sad about us.

There are many ways to show love and respect for our parents and other caring adults. We may not always feel like doing this. We may feel tired, angry, or unhappy, or we may have other important things to think about. But God calls us to show love and respect for all those people who care for us.

Activity

Read these stories. Then write endings that show how the child in each story followed the fourth commandment.

1. One afternoon Alex waited and waited for his mother to pick him up at the bus stop. He felt angrier with each passing minute. When his mother finally arrived, Alex screamed at her for making him wait so long. He got in the car and slammed the door. Neither one said a word all the way home. Alex went straight to his room. Before supper he went to his mother and

   _____

   _____

   _____

2. "You are not to cross the street except when the light is green," Joan's father ordered. "Do you understand?" Joan nodded her head. The next day, Joan was in a hurry coming home from a science fair at school. She was on her bicycle. She did not want to stop at a very busy corner. The light was red and Joan could see cars coming. But she thought that she would have plenty of time to cross the street if she pedaled faster. Then Joan remembered what her father had told her. Joan decided to

   _____

   _____

   _____

Praying a Family Blessing

Blessings are an important part of our faith as Catholics. We have blessings for people and pets. We have blessings for meals, objects, and places. Our blessings praise God and ask that certain gifts such as faith and trust be given to us.

Read the blessing for families below. Then on the lines provided, write a prayer of blessing for your family.

A Family Blessing

May the Lord Jesus,
who lived with his holy family in Nazareth,
dwell also with our family,
keep it from all evil,
and make all of us one in heart and mind.
Amen.

My Family Blessing

_____

_____

_____

_____

_____

Chapter Review

Fill in the blanks to find the missing words. Then write these words in the puzzle below. You will find one word that sums up the fourth commandment.

1. When our parents are in need, we should ____ ____ ____ ____ them.

2. We should ____ ____ ____ ____ our parents.

3. We should pray for our ____ ____ ____ ____ ____ ____ ____.

4. Giving gifts is one way of showing ____ ____ ____ ____ for our parents.

5. We show ____ ____ ____ ____ ____ ____ ____ for our parents by speaking kindly to them.

Answer the first two questions on the lines provided.

1. What is meant by *honor*?

   _____

2. What does the fourth commandment teach us?

   _____

   _____

3. Discuss how we can obey the fourth commandment.

Children, obey your parents.
Based on Ephesians 6:1

11

Respecting Life

How do you feel when someone does not treat you well and hurts you with their words or actions?

Activity

The cartoon above tells a story about what happened one day in school when some fourth graders were asked by their teacher to be kind to a student who didn't have any friends.

1. If you had been a part of the conversation in the cartoon, what comment would you make?

_____

_____

_____

_____

2. Would you change your behavior toward the boy, or would you let others worry about him?

_____

_____

_____

_____

Understanding the Fifth Commandment

Jesus lived nonviolently all his life. He had great respect and love for all living things. Most of all, he loved people and respected human life. He healed people instead of hurting them. He became angry at evil and injustice, but he did not fight or kill. He took the side of the weak and helped those whom others avoided and looked down on.

The fifth commandment is *You shall not kill.* Jesus lived by the fifth commandment. He wants us to live by it, too.

The fifth commandment calls us to respect all living beings. It teaches us that all life is **sacred**. We are to care for ourselves and our health. We must work against **violence** and help those who have been hurt. If we follow the fifth commandment, we will work to protect all life.

Vocabulary

sacred: entitled to respect; holy

violence: rough or harmful actions or words

We Believe

The fifth commandment teaches us to respect and care for all living things. It teaches us that all life is sacred.

Put Away Your Sword

It was dark in the garden of Gethsemane. Jesus went there to pray. Peter, James, and John were with him.

Suddenly Jesus and his disciples heard people walking. They heard angry voices coming closer. A crowd of men rushed into the garden. They carried swords and clubs. Jesus' friends were surprised and afraid.

Judas, one of Jesus' disciples, was part of the mob. He walked up to Jesus and hugged him. This was a sign to the others that Jesus was the man they wanted.

Some men grabbed Jesus and held his arms. One of the disciples had a sword. He pulled it out and struck at one of the men who held Jesus. He cut off the man's ear.

But Jesus said to his disciple, "Put your sword back where it belongs. Those who use the sword will be destroyed by it."

The mob then took Jesus off into the darkness.

Based on Matthew 26:36–37; 47–52

Activity

Think about the meaning of Jesus' words in the Scripture story you just read. On the lines below, write why you think Jesus told his disciple to put his sword away.

_____

_____

_____

What might you have done if you had been in Jesus' place?

_____

_____

Jesus, Our Model of Nonviolence

The disciples had seen many other examples of Jesus' nonviolence. Later, after Jesus died and had risen from the dead, they understood even more.

The Bible tells us of a time when a crowd of people attacked a woman. They were going to kill her by throwing stones at her. Jesus stopped them.

Even throughout his suffering and death, Jesus remained nonviolent. He never fought back. He never called for his followers to come and fight for him.

Jesus' message of nonviolence is the same message we hear today. Jesus calls us to settle our differences peacefully, to avoid fighting and other forms of violence, and to treat all people with gentleness and kindness.

Rahjid's Dilemma

Rahjid came to the United States from India when he was eleven years old. At his new school, the principal put him in the third grade because she knew it would be difficult for him to keep up with his own class. There were so many new things to learn, especially English! Because he was older and bigger than his classmates, Rahjid found it hard to make friends. His younger brother was having problems being accepted by his classmates, too.

Children in school made fun of the way Rahjid and his brother dressed and the way they spoke. Children in their neighborhood called them bad names. But Rahjid's parents had taught the boys never to use violence to solve a problem. So, even when Rahjid felt angry and hurt, he never reacted with violent words or actions.

On the playground one day, two boys began teasing and shoving Rahjid's younger brother. They were going to take his new jacket from him. By the time Rahjid rushed to his brother's side, the boys had already pushed the young boy down. Rahjid's brother was frightened and crying. Rahjid was furious! Rahjid was bigger and stronger than the boys who were bullying his brother. He could easily shove them around and hurt them. He thought for a moment about what to do.

Discuss

What do you think Rahjid did?
Why do you think Rahjid made this decision?

Called to Respect All Life

The fifth commandment *You shall not kill* means much more than not taking someone's life. It means showing respect for human life. When we care about our health, we are keeping the fifth commandment. When we avoid hitting or pushing others, we are also keeping the fifth commandment.

When we stop being respectful of people and other living things, we move toward violent words and actions. Violent words and actions are hurtful and disrespectful of others.

We are called to keep the fifth commandment as Jesus did. Jesus always respected people because he knew that all people are made in God's image.

Activity

Some violent actions are listed below. For each violent action, write an opposite, peaceful action.

Making fun of others _____

Lying about someone _____

Using hurtful words _____

Pushing or shoving others _____

Starting fights _____

Trying to injure someone _____

Taking someone's life _____

Activity

Various kinds of violence and abuse are shown on TV. What are your three favorite TV programs? List the shows' titles below. Then check the box next to each show title to rate how often you think violence and abuse are shown on that show.

TV Violence

	Never	Sometimes	A lot
Show Number **1** _____	☐	☐	☐
Show Number **2** _____	☐	☐	☐
Show Number **3** _____	☐	☐	☐

Love Your Enemies ~~~

One day while Jesus was teaching a large group of people, he said something that was very surprising.

"I tell you this, love your enemies. Do good to those who dislike you. Use only words of blessing on those who curse you. Pray for those who treat you badly.

"If a person slaps you on one cheek, offer the person your other cheek also. And if a person steals your coat, give that person your shirt as well. Share everything you have with those who ask you. And if a person wrongfully takes what belongs to you, don't ask for it back.

"Do to other people what you would want other people to do to you."

Based on Luke 6:27–31

Violence in Our World

Even in our everyday lives, violence and **abuse** occur all around us. Rough and dangerous actions can hurt us physically. Hateful and unkind words can hurt us emotionally.

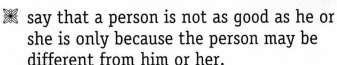

People are violent when they

* use words like "shut up!" or "I hate you!"
* call other people names or hurt the feelings of others.
* ignore someone or keep someone out of the group.

* say that a person is not as good as he or she is only because the person may be different from him or her.
* tell lies about others.
* threaten and bully others.
* try to cause physical harm to others or to the property of others.

Activity

Name the violent actions that you think most fourth graders struggle with.

1. _____

2. _____

Now name one way you can avoid violence in your life.

_____

_____

Praying the Way of the Cross

The Way (or Stations) of the Cross is a traditional devotion most often prayed during the season of Lent. It recalls the suffering, death, and resurrection of Jesus. There are many different ways we can pray the Way of the Cross. We can pray this devotion alone or with others. Decide with your teacher and classmates how your class can pray the Way of the Cross.

1. Jesus is condemned to death.

2. Jesus accepts the cross.

3. Jesus falls the first time.

4. Jesus meets his mother.

5. Simon helps Jesus carry the cross.

6. Veronica wipes the face of Jesus.

7. Jesus falls the second time.

8. Jesus meets the women of Jerusalem.

9. Jesus falls the third time.

10. Jesus is stripped of his clothes.

11. Jesus is nailed to the cross.

12. Jesus dies on the cross.

13. Jesus is taken down from the cross.

14. Jesus is buried in the tomb.

15. Jesus rises from the dead.

Chapter Review

Check **Yes** if the fifth commandment is being followed. Check **No** if it is not.

Yes   No

1. ☐ ☐ Mr. Harris speeds through a red light to get to work on time.

2. ☐ ☐ Lee Ann keeps her body healthy. She eats foods that are good for her.

3. ☐ ☐ Henry hits someone whom he doesn't like.

4. ☐ ☐ A country starts a war to take over another country.

5. ☐ ☐ Amy is kind to someone who has no friends.

6. ☐ ☐ Doug and Tom take drugs that can hurt them.

7. ☐ ☐ Keneisha and her friends make fun of Margarita because she speaks with an accent.

On the lines provided, write your answers to the first two questions.

1. What is *violence*?

_____

_____

2. What does the fifth commandment teach us?

_____

_____

_____

_____

Jesus says, "Learn from me for I am gentle."
Based on Matthew 11:29

3. Discuss how we can obey the fifth commandment.

12

Being Faithful in Marriage

What makes someone a good friend? What do friends do for one another?

Activity

Think of your friends. Then read each of the following statements that show how people are friends with others. Add one more statement you think is also important.

- We have fun together.
- We share secrets.
- We are important to each other.
- We help each other.
- We trust each other.
- We are honest with each other.
- We stand up for each other.

- We _____.

A Faithful Friend

The Bible tells us in the Book of Genesis that people are not meant to be lonely. We read that God created people so that no one would be alone.

The Bible also tells us how important friends are. We read,

"A **faithful** friend is a strong shelter; whoever finds one finds a treasure."

"A faithful friend is more valuable than anything; no money can equal what a friend is worth" (based on Sirach 6:14–15).

Activity

Think about one of your best friends. Design a friendship T-shirt for him or her. Use words and symbols to show on it what friendship means to you. Use the extra space on the right for any extra symbols or words.

Vocabulary

faithful: able to be trusted and depended upon

Activity

Answer the following question about faithfulness, and then complete the sentences.

1. What does faithfulness mean to you?

_____

_____

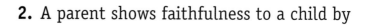

2. A parent shows faithfulness to a child by

_____

3. A teacher shows faithfulness to a student by

_____

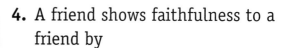

4. A friend shows faithfulness to a friend by

_____

5. A child shows faithfulness to a parent by

_____

Called to Faithfulness and Respect

The sacrament of Matrimony celebrates the love between a man and a woman. Love in marriage is a sharing between two people. As married people, they promise to love each other and to share their lives together.

God gives us two commandments to teach us about the love between a husband and a wife. They are the sixth and ninth commandments.

The sixth commandment is *You shall not commit* **adultery**.
The ninth commandment is *You shall not* **covet** *your neighbor's wife.*

Through the sixth and ninth commandments we learn that two married people are to be faithful to each other. They are to love and respect each other.

These two commandments call all of us to respect the gift of our sexuality. Our bodies and our sexuality are gifts from God that help us express our love for others and to feel their love for us.

Activity

We can show respect for each other and for ourselves in many ways. Name some of the ways you show respect for others and yourself every day.

_____

_____

_____

_____

_____

_____

_____

_____

_____

Vocabulary

adultery: being unfaithful to one's husband or wife by giving to someone else the special love promised in marriage

covet: to want something someone else has

We Believe

The sixth and ninth commandments call married people to love each other and live together faithfully.

A Special Love

Sometimes a man and a woman are in love and want to spend their lives together.

They decide to marry and invite their families and friends to their wedding.

At the wedding, they promise to be faithful to one another for the rest of their lives. They promise to love one another.

As they hold hands, they each say, "I promise to be true to you in good times and in bad, in sickness and in health. I will love you and honor you all the days of my life" (Consent, *Rite of Marriage*). The man and woman are now married. They are husband and wife.

They each place a ring on the other's finger and say, "Take this ring as a sign of my love and fidelity" (Blessing of Rings, *Rite of Marriage*).

The priest blesses them. The priest prays that they will always live together in love. He asks God to help them be faithful friends and marriage partners.

"Father," the priest prays, "keep them always true to your commandments. Keep them faithful in marriage and let them be living examples of Christian life" (Nuptial Blessing, *Rite of Marriage*).

Activity

Complete the sentences below with examples of how the married couples can show love, faithfulness, and respect.

1. José and Elena have been married for twelve years. José has just lost his job and doesn't know how he will support his family.

Elena could _____

_____

_____ .

2. Sean and Sarah are newlyweds. Sean is often out of town on business. Sarah goes to her job each day and takes care of her

elderly mother. Sean could _____

_____

_____ .

Activity

Examine these photographs. Write one thing the husbands and wives are sharing with each other and with others.

▲ _____

_____

▲ _____

_____

◀ _____

_____

Reaching Out to Others

Married people are called to live out their promises of faithfulness. In doing so, they share many things together. God also asks married people to reach out to others. They are expected to share their belongings and their time with others. The more that married couples and all good friends care about each other, the more they tend to reach out to others.

A Loving Marriage

Margaret was a beautiful princess. But her beauty was no protection in time of war. When the armies of William the Conqueror invaded England, Margaret and her brother tried to leave, but they became shipwrecked. They both survived and were taken to the palace of King Malcolm of Scotland.

The king immediately fell in love with the beautiful princess. Margaret soon came to love the king, and agreed to marry him.

In the years that followed, Malcolm and Margaret had a large family—six sons and two daughters—whom they loved very much. The king and queen loved each other, too. They traveled together. They often prayed together. They did many good things for the people of Scotland.

Malcolm and Margaret often left their palace to visit the poor and to care for the sick. During Advent and Lent, hundreds of needy people went to the palace for help. Malcolm and Margaret gave them food, money, and medicine.

The king and queen had been happily married for twenty-three years at their deaths, just a few days apart, in A.D. 1093.

Catholics honor Margaret as a saint and patroness of Scotland. November 16 is the feast day of Saint Margaret.

Discuss

What were two of the ways Margaret and Malcolm reached out to others?

Praying for Faithfulness

When a man and a woman celebrate the sacrament of Matrimony, their family and friends come to the wedding to pray with them. Together they listen to Scripture and pray for God's gift of faithfulness for themselves and for the newly married couple. They might listen to the Scripture reading below about love and faithfulness.

> Love is patient, love is kind. It is not jealous. Love is not proud or self-centered. It is not rude or selfish. Love is not quick-tempered, it does not dwell on injury. Love does not rejoice over wrongdoing, but rejoices with goodness. Love bears all things, believes all things, hopes all things, endures all things. Love never fails.
>
> *Based on 1 Corinthians 13:4–8*

Activity

Complete the prayer below, asking God to help you be a more loving and faithful person.

Faithfulness ♥ Faithfulness ♥ Faithfulness

Dear God,
Help me be a loving and faithful son/daughter by _____
_____.

Help me be a faithful friend by _____
_____.

Help me show my love and faithfulness to you by _____
_____.

I ask your help through Jesus, your Son. Amen.

Chapter Review

What are two things a husband and wife promise each other?

1. ____ ____ ____ ____

2. ____ ____ ____ ____ ____ ____ ____ ____ ____ ____ ____ ____ ____

List three ways you show respect for your own body.

1. _____

2. _____

3. _____

List the promises a man and a woman make to each other in the sacrament of Matrimony.

_____

_____

_____

On the lines provided, write your answer to the first two questions.

1. What is meant by *faithful*?

_____

2. What do the sixth and ninth commandments teach us?

_____

_____

_____

3. Discuss how friends can be faithful.

I will marry you in faithfulness.
Based on Hosea 2:21–22

UNIT **3** ORGANIZER

Respecting God and People

Complete the unit organizer by supplying important words or phrases that describe the commandment or commandments you learned about in each chapter.

Chapter 10

The fourth commandment

_____
_____
_____
_____

Chapter 9

The first three commandments

_____
_____
_____

Chapter 12

The sixth and ninth commandments

Chapter 11 The fifth commandment

_____
_____
_____
_____

_____
_____
_____

UNIT 3 REVIEW

Match the words in Column A with the definition in Column B.

Column A   **Column B**

1. in vain   _____ an attitude of respect and care

2. honor   _____ to want something someone else has

3. violence   _____ in a disrespectful way

4. reverence   _____ rough or harmful action

5. faithful   _____ able to be trusted and depended upon

6. covet   _____ to treat with respect

Identify the number of the commandment described in each sentence.

1. _____ We honor God in a special way each Sunday.

2. _____ Married people love each other and live together faithfully.

3. _____ We place God first in our lives.

4. _____ We love and obey our parents.

5. _____ We use God's name with respect.

6. _____ We respect and care for all human beings.

Write a brief answer to each question.

1. Which day of the week is the Christian Sabbath? _____

2. How did Jesus live by the fifth commandment?

_____

3. How can we honor our parents and others who care for us?

_____

_____

Find the hidden words in the puzzle and circle them.

NAZARETH
MARY
WISER
PRAYED
OBEYED
PRAISED
COMMANDMENT
LEARNED
HEALTHY
FAMILY

```
F C A R P E N T E R A R B C G
O Y G S Q N A G O B E U L O X
S F H T O L Z O B H C K O M L
T A U G H T A P E E X O V M E
P R A Y E D R L Y L S S E A A
R P R A I S E D E P T A D N R
F A M I L Y T X D E R B W D N
A J O S E P H Z W D O B L M E
P D W I S E R D Q P N A N E D
H A P P Y R Z K G Y G T W N R
E H E A L T H Y O Z E H V T K
B L T H A N K E D X R M A R Y
```

JOSEPH
CARPENTER
TAUGHT
SABBATH
GOD
THANKED
LOVED
HAPPY
HELPED
STRONGER

Write **True** or **False** for each sentence.

1. A faithful friend is like a treasure. _____

2. In marriage a woman and a man promise to be faithful to one another. _____

3. The fourth and fifth commandments teach us about marriage. _____

4. Husbands and wives need God's help to keep their promise to love one another. _____

5. Margaret, the queen of Scotland, refused to let the poor people into her home. _____

6. All violent behavior is against the fifth commandment. _____

7. The commandments are meant to take away our fun. _____

8. The fourth commandment tells us to have respect for our own bodies. _____

PRACTICING MAKING GOOD CHOICES

Activity

Match the following moral decision-making terms with their definitions by writing the correct numbers on the lines in front of the definitions.

1. moral choice   _____ **a.** lives life like Jesus

2. conscience   _____ **b.** uncertain about what is right and wrong

3. consequence   _____ **c.** a choice between what is right and wrong

4. asking for advice   _____ **d.** the power to decide what is right and wrong

5. prayer   _____ **e.** a way to ask Jesus for help

6. follower of Jesus   _____ **f.** what happens as a result of your choice

7. moral dilemma   _____ **g.** seeking help with a decision

On the lines below, write about a moral dilemma you are facing, or a situation in which you are uncertain about the right thing to do.

_____

_____

_____

_____

_____

_____

_____

Using the dilemma you have described and the Steps for Making Good Choices from page 56, decide what might be the right thing to do.

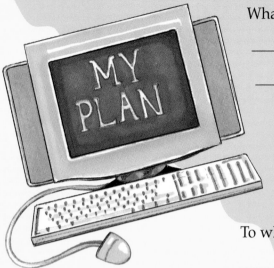

What do you think you should do? Why?

_____

_____

What are two possible consequences?

_____

_____

To whom might you go for advice?

_____

_____

Does your decision show you are a follower of Jesus? Why or why not?

_____

_____

If your choice does not show you to be a follower of Jesus, what else could you do?

_____

_____

Following Jesus

Jesus is always with us, especially in times of doubt or when we are faced with difficult choices. Jesus has given us the Holy Spirit to help us know what is right and to have the courage to act in ways that show we are his followers.

PRAYER

Jesus, for all the times I've said no to what I knew was the right thing to do, forgive me. For all the times I've encouraged others to do wrong, forgive me. Amen.

OPENING DOORS
A Take-Home Magazine™

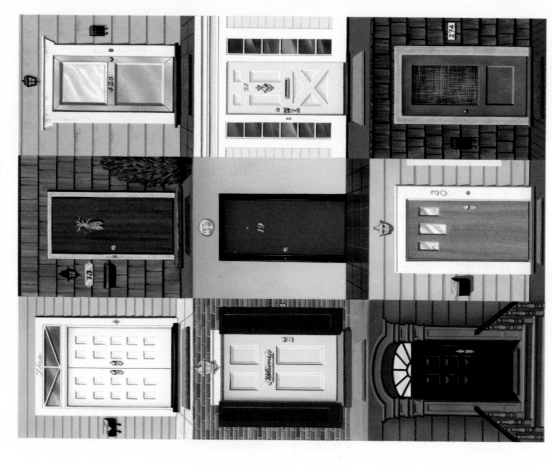

THIS IS OUR FAITH

Growing Closer

RECLAIM Saturday evenings and Sundays, the Christian Sabbath, as time for celebration and re-creation. Even if someone has to work, try to plan one special hour together.

Be sure everyone feels free to make suggestions. Try to include in your plans at least one idea from each family member. Plan to do things that increase respect for one another as fellow travelers of faith.

Looking Ahead

Unit 4 will focus on the seventh, eighth, and tenth commandments, which promote respect for the truth and the property of others. These commandments are based on attitudes of honesty, trust, and concern for the rights of others that your fourth grader needs in order to develop a responsive and responsible conscience. The unit also deals with the mercy and forgiveness of God and others.

8

Faithful Companions

In the Preview of THIS IS OUR FAITH, you were invited to continue on the faith journey with your child. The comparison of maturing in faith with making a journey is one that is comfortably well used and worn.

All those who make the faith journey reach some bend or fork in the road when they realize that they need a scout, guide, or companion to continue. You are being asked to be your child's guide. It may be helpful to remember that God, ever vigilant and faithful, is there to help you. The Ten Commandments, the Great Commandment, and the Beatitudes are maps and guideposts along the way.

Your ways, O LORD, make known to me;
 teach me your paths,
Guide me in your truth and teach me,
 for you are God my savior,
 and for you I wait all the day.

Psalm 25:4-5

I will instruct you and show you the way you should walk;
I will counsel you, keeping my eye on you.

Psalm 32:8

He set my feet upon a crag;
 he made firm my steps.
And he put a new song into my mouth,
 a hymn to our God.

Psalm 40:3-4

SONGS for Christ's Followers

The Book of Psalms in the Old Testament, also called the Hebrew Scriptures, contains prayers and songs from the time of King David and after (1000 B.C. to 400 B.C.). Priests and scribes put the psalms together to use in the Temple in Jerusalem after their time of exile.

There are different types of psalms, including the following: hymns of praise and thanksgiving, psalms of wisdom that chart ways to happiness, songs to honor the king, and prayers to petition God's help in time of sickness, war, and death.

In many of the psalms, the writers used journey or traveling images. Some of these poetic words are on page 7. You and your family may want to think about and pray these words on your faith journey. You may also want to read the entire psalm in the Bible.

The LORD is my shepherd; I shall not want
    In verdant pastures he gives me repose;
    Beside restful waters he leads me;
    he refreshes my soul.
    He guides me in right paths
    for his name's sake.

Psalm 23:1-3

Excess Baggage

Product developers are constantly researching ways to make luggage lighter and easier to carry. Wrinkle-free clothing has been discovered and travel irons and alarm clocks have been sold for a long time. The business of travel is so popular and extensive that now even special instructors teach people how to pack.

In your role as guide for your family's journey of faith, you may need to teach the younger members how to pack. Use the story of the rich young man (Mark 10:17–22) to illustrate your points about possessions and priorities. In light of that story and the Beatitudes (Matthew 5:1–6), discuss what your family considers excess baggage.

4

CHRIST OUR LIGHT

Our journey of faith begins at Baptism. After a child has been baptized, someone in the family lights a small candle from the flame of the Easter candle and the celebrant prays the following prayer.

"Parents and godparents, this light is entrusted to you to be kept burning brightly. This child of yours has been enlightened by Christ. He (she) is to walk always as a child of light. May he (she) keep the flame of faith alive in his (her) heart. When the Lord comes, may he (she) go out to meet him with all the saints in the heavenly kingdom."

The Rite of Baptism

To help us continue to walk as children of light and to keep the flame of faith alive in our hearts, the Church reminds us during the liturgical year of Christ's light. This happens particularly during the service of light at the Easter Vigil.

The priest blesses the new fire, which is started outside.

Father,
we share in the light of your glory
through your son, the light of the world.
Make this new fire ✷ holy, and inflame us with new hope.
Purify our minds by this Easter celebration
and bring us one day to the feast of eternal light.

After the Easter candle is lit from the new fire, the priest then prays the following words.

May the light of Christ, rising in glory,
dispel the darkness of our hearts and minds.

Daily, you help to dispel the darkness by teaching and guiding as a parent and chasing away gloom and depression with a smile, a hug, or words of comfort and cheer.

5

Respecting
Truth and
Property

How do you feel about someone who lies about you or steals from you?

13

Respecting What Belongs to Others

Think of the last time you wanted something you couldn't have. How did you feel?

Andy's Greed

Andy and Nicole were neighbors. They were also good friends. Nicole and Andy often played in Nicole's house.

Andy's parents bought Andy some hand-held computer games for his birthday, but they did not get the one that Andy really wanted. The game he liked best was the one that Nicole had.

"I wish I had Nicole's computer game," Andy thought to himself. "It's the most fun."

Andy dreamed about having Nicole's computer game. He thought about how he could get one just like it. He could not ask his parents for it, because they had just given him some games. So Andy decided to take Nicole's game the next time he went to her house.

The next day Andy was at Nicole's house. Nicole's mother called her out of the room. While Nicole was with her mother, Andy took Nicole's game. Then Andy yelled to Nicole that he had to go home. Andy was in such a hurry to leave that he fell as he ran down the front sidewalk, dropping the computer game. He picked both himself and the game up quickly and ran to his house.

Andy's mother and father were not home from work yet, so Andy sat down to play the game. He tried and tried, but it did not work. Something was wrong. Andy looked carefully at the game. It must have been damaged when he dropped it.

"What will I do now?" Andy wondered.

Greed in Our Lives

All that God has created in the world is good. Through God's generosity we have been given many gifts. But sometimes we want more and more things. Sometimes we want more than we need. This is called **greed**.

Though we may have what we need, we may sometimes want what someone else has. We may even want it so much that we take it from the other person. Wanting something that belongs to another is called **envy**.

When we are not willing to share what we have with others, we are being selfish. Wanting to keep everything for ourselves is never right.

Vocabulary

greed: wanting more and more things when they are not needed

envy: wanting something that belongs to another

◆ ◆ ◆ ◆ ◆ ◆ ◆ ◆ ◆ ◆ ◆ ◆

The Commandments of Sharing

When Jesus was teaching, he knew that some people were filled with greed. They wanted more than they already had. They would **cheat**, or trick, other people to get what they wanted. Jesus also knew that some people were full of envy. They wanted the good things that belonged to others. And Jesus knew that sometimes people did not share what they had with the poor.

God gives us two rules, or commandments, to teach us that everyone has a right to the things they need to live happy, healthy lives. They are the seventh and tenth commandments.

The seventh commandment is *You shall not steal.*

The tenth commandment is *You shall not covet anything that belongs to your neighbor.*

All of God's gifts are meant for everyone. We are called to show that we are grateful for God's gifts by caring for what we have and sharing our gifts with others. We should not take what belongs to others. We should not cheat others out of what is theirs or waste anything that God has made. We are asked to fight against envy and greed in our hearts. We should be thankful for the good things we have been given.

Activity

| steal | selfishness | envy | greed | cheat |

Write the correct word on each line.

1. Wanting more and more things

   _____

2. To get something from someone in a dishonest way

   _____

3. Wanting to keep everything for yourself

   _____

4. Wanting something that belongs to another

   _____

5. To take something that belongs to another

Do I Respect the Property of Others?

The seventh and tenth commandments tell us that we must respect the property of others. Ask yourself the following questions to discover what kinds of actions go against these commandments.

1. *We do not respect the property of others if we are wasteful.* Do I waste paper or school supplies? Do I waste food or other things that belong to my family?

2. *We do not respect the property of others if we are careless.* Am I careless with things others allow me to use? Am I careless with materials I use at school?

3. *We do not respect the property of others if we purposely cause harm or damage to something.* Do I write on walls or desks? Do I write in books or tear the pages? Do I ruin something that belongs to another because I am envious or angry?

4. *We do not respect the property of others if we try to cheat others.* Do I try to trick younger children into giving me their things? Do I try to cheat others out of their belongings?

5. *We do not respect the property of others if we take what belongs to someone else.* Do I take things that belong to others without permission? Do I cheat on tests? Do I keep things I find without trying to find the owner? Do I take anything in a store without paying for it? Do I copy homework from other students?

Activity

Write what the person in each story can do to follow the seventh and tenth commandments.

1. Dolores is with her mother and little brother in the grocery store. Dolores likes cherries. While her mother's back is turned, Dolores goes to the fruit section to find the cherries. She could take some and eat them.

Dolóres should _____

_____

_____ .

2. Peter's mother always makes a lunch for him to take to school. He doesn't want the apple that his mother put in his lunch. He could just throw it out.

Or Peter could _____

_____

_____ .

3. Mrs. Williams works in an office. There is a closet filled with office supplies. Her children always need paper, pens, and pencils for school. She can remove the supplies from the office supply closet and then take them home. No one will know that they are missing. But Mrs. Williams knows that this is wrong.

Mrs. Williams should _____

_____ .

Activity

Sometimes it is difficult to share what we have with others. Complete the sentences to find out what you think about sharing.

1. The three things that are the most difficult for me to share are

   _____

   _____

   _____ .

2. The three things that are the easiest for me to

   share are _____

   _____

   _____ .

The Rich Man and Lazarus 〜〜

One day, Jesus told this story.

"Once there was a rich man. He lived in a big house, and he dressed in the finest clothes. He and his family ate the best food every day.

"At the rich man's door," Jesus went on, "lay a man named Lazarus. He was sick and covered with sores. He was so hungry that he wanted to eat the scraps that fell from the rich man's table. Dogs even came to lick his sores.

"The rich man hardly noticed Lazarus and never gave him anything," Jesus said. "The beggar died and went to live with God. The rich man died, too, but he went to a place of suffering. When the rich man looked up in his pain, he could see Lazarus happy with God."

Based on Luke 16:19–23

Jesus Teaches Us About Sharing

Jesus' story tells us that those who have the good things of life must share them with those who are in real need. Even if we do not have much, we are still expected to share what we have with others. God created the world and all that is in it for the good of everyone.

Activity

Below are ten reasons or excuses why people are either willing or unwilling to share what they have. Read each sentence and then put a ✓ in the appropriate column.

		WILLING	UNWILLING
1.	People won't appreciate what I give them.	☐	☐
2.	God has made all things for the good of everyone.	☐	☐
3.	Jesus tells us that we must share what we have with others.	☐	☐
4.	I won't have enough for myself.	☐	☐
5.	God has been good to me, so I will share what I have.	☐	☐
6.	Other people don't really need anything from me.	☐	☐
7.	They won't take care of what I give them.	☐	☐
8.	I deserve what I have; others don't.	☐	☐
9.	I don't really need as much as I have.	☐	☐
10.	I don't have much, but you can have some.	☐	☐

Praying with Gratitude

God has given each of us so much for which we can be thankful. Prayers of thanks or gratitude are important prayers because these prayers remind us that it is *God* who is responsible for all the good things in our lives. We remember God's goodness and give thanks.

Make a list of ten people, places, or things for which you are thankful. Then use your list to join your class in praying a prayer of gratitude.

God, our Creator, I thank you for

_____

_____

_____

_____

_____

_____

_____

_____

_____

_____

Chapter Review

Six words in the list below relate to keeping the seventh and tenth commandments. Write these words on the lines provided.

waste	share	envy	care	steal	respect	greedy	harm	lie
unselfish	cheat	generous	truthful	fight	covet	gossip

_____   _____

_____   _____

_____   _____

Write your answers to the first two questions on the lines provided.

1. What is meant by *greed*?

_____

2. Why are the seventh and tenth commandments so important?

_____

_____

_____

_____

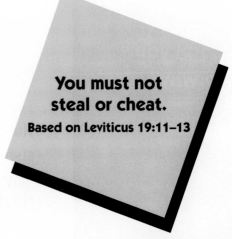

You must not steal or cheat.
Based on Leviticus 19:11–13

3. Discuss how we can better follow the seventh commandment.

14

Respecting the Truth

Was there a time when you told a lie about someone? How did you feel? Why?

Activity

Read the following stories. For each story, talk about who was hurt because the truth was not told. Also, tell how each person was hurt.

1. Everyone in the class knew that Suzie's watch had been taken from her locker. Maggie had no idea who had taken it. But she was angry at Joanne and did not like her. So Maggie whispered to Greg, "Joanne took Suzie's watch." Greg told June. June told Chen. Soon everyone believed that Joanne had taken Suzie's watch.

2. For homework, Charles had to write a story about fish. He had no ideas. Then he found a book about fish in his sister's bedroom. Charles copied the story and titled it "My Fish Story." Charles gave his homework to his teacher. She knew right away that it was not Charles' work because she also had the same book.

Lying Hurts Others

Lying always hurts someone. When we tell lies about another person, the person gets hurt. Sometimes even the family or the friends of the person can be hurt by our lies.

When we lie, we hurt ourselves by doing something that is wrong and we lose the trust of our friends and families. Afterward, they may no longer believe us, even when we tell the truth. We may begin with one lie, but soon we may be telling more lies.

Jesus teaches us to be truthful. We need to be truly honest. Others need to know that we can be trusted. They want to know that they can believe what we say.

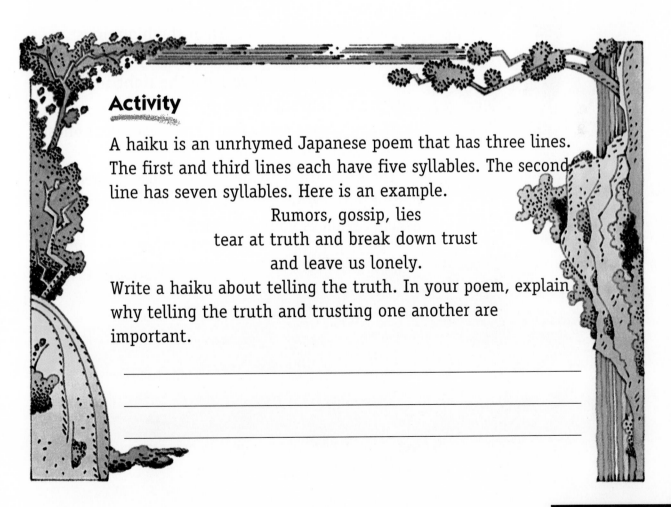

Activity

A haiku is an unrhymed Japanese poem that has three lines. The first and third lines each have five syllables. The second line has seven syllables. Here is an example.

Rumors, gossip, lies
tear at truth and break down trust
and leave us lonely.

Write a haiku about telling the truth. In your poem, explain why telling the truth and trusting one another are important.

_____

_____

_____

False Witnesses

Jesus told the truth even when people lied about him. Jesus told the truth even when he knew it would lead to his death.

It was night. The men had taken Jesus from the Garden of Gethsemane. They led him to the home of the **high priest**, a powerful leader of the Temple.

Some other Temple leaders were gathered at the high priest's house. They were trying to find a reason to put Jesus to death, but they could not agree. Some people told lies about Jesus, but their stories did not agree.

Finally, the high priest stood up before everyone. He questioned Jesus.

"Have you no answer to what these men say about you?" the high priest asked.

Jesus did not answer. Then the high priest became angry. He asked Jesus, "Do you think you are God's messiah and so have the right to criticize us in front of the people?"

"I am," Jesus said. Jesus knew that his honest answer would lead to his death.

The high priest turned to all those gathered before him. "What more do you need to hear?" he asked. "What is your decision?"

"Jesus is guilty!" they all shouted.

Based on Mark 14:53–64

The Eighth Commandment

Jesus' example and words teach us how to live. Jesus does not want us to **bear false witness** against one another. He does not want us to lie. Jesus says, "Say yes when you mean yes and no when you mean no. Anything other than that is a lie" (based on Matthew 5:37). Jesus also says, "If you live by my teaching, you will know the truth. The truth will set you free" (based on John 8:31–32).

Jesus lived by the eighth commandment. He wants us to live by it, too. The eighth commandment is *You shall not bear false witness against your neighbor.*

The eighth commandment teaches that God wants us to respect the truth. God does not want us to lie to others or about others or to spread false rumors or harmful gossip.

Activity

Finish the following sentences with ideas you think are possibilities for fourth graders.

1. Instead of lying about how I did on the math test, I could

   _____.

2. Instead of gossiping about the clothes that someone is wearing, I could

   _____.

3. Instead of telling lies about someone I don't like, I could

   _____

   _____

   _____.

Vocabulary

high priest: a powerful leader of the Temple at the time of Jesus

bear false witness: to tell a lie

◆◆◆◆◆◆◆◆◆◆◆◆

We Believe

God calls us to respect the truth. When we lie, we hurt ourselves and others.

An Honest Man

Franz Jaegerstaetter was a farmer in Austria during very difficult and dangerous times. He and his wife, Francesca, had three daughters. Franz worked hard on the farm to support his family.

In 1933, Hitler and the Nazi party came to power in Germany. Jaegerstaetter was convinced that the Nazi movement was evil and said so openly. Five years later the German Nazis took over Austria.

All Austrians had to vote whether or not they approved of the Nazi occupation. Knowing the consequences, Jaegerstaetter voted no. He said that it would be a lie for him to approve of what he believed was evil.

In 1943, Jaegerstaetter received an order to join the army, which was under Nazi control. He would have to take an oath, agreeing to Nazi beliefs. His family and friends urged him to do so. For him that would have been telling a lie.

He was arrested and put in prison. Fellow prisoners remembered how he prayed in his cell and shared the little food he had with others. He wrote to his wife and daughters, and he urged them always to tell the truth, no matter what the cost.

At his trial, Jaegerstaetter still refused to enter the army. For him, to have worn the uniform would have been to live a lie. He was condemned to death.

After a final visit from his wife and pastor, on August 8, 1943, Franz Jaegerstaetter gave his life for the truth. Even in the last moments of his life, Franz refused to lie.

Being an Honest Person

The story of Franz Jaegerstaetter reminds us that it is not always easy to be an honest person. Although Franz was an adult with a difficult choice to make, fourth graders too can be challenged to be honest and truthful.

To help you be an honest person, you should remember that to bear false witness is always wrong, even if

- a friend asks you to lie for him or her.
- friends gossip or spread rumors about others.
- a lie would keep someone out of trouble.
- a lie would be an easy way out of a predicament.

You should always be honest even if

- telling the truth would get a friend into trouble.
- telling the truth would get you into trouble.
- telling the truth would be embarrassing.

God asks us always to respect the truth and to live by the eighth commandment.

Activity

Using words and one or more images, create a newspaper ad that might "sell" the importance of telling the truth. You may use anything in the lesson, as well as your own convictions, to create the ad.

After each statement, put a ✓ in the column that tells what might be true for people your age.

YES	NO		
☐	☐	**1.**	We will lie for a friend if he or she asks.
☐	☐	**2.**	We will lie to keep ourselves or a friend out of trouble.
☐	☐	**3.**	We tell the truth even if it is embarrassing.
☐	☐	**4.**	We spread rumors and gossip among our friends.
☐	☐	**5.**	People can always believe what we tell them.

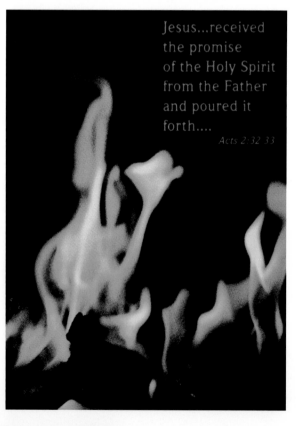

Jesus...received the promise of the Holy Spirit from the Father and poured it forth....
Acts 2:32 33

I Will Send You the Holy Spirit

When Jesus went to Jerusalem to eat the Passover Supper with his friends for the last time, he gathered them around himself at the table.

He said, "The Father will send the Spirit to you in my name. The Holy Spirit will teach you even more and remind you of everything I have already taught you."

Jesus continued, "I have much more to tell you but it is too much for you to hear all at once. But when the Spirit of Truth comes to you, you will be guided to the truth."

Based on John 14:26; 16:12–13

The Holy Spirit Helps Us

God has given us the gift of the Holy Spirit. We believe that the Spirit helps us to live in truth. We can always ask the Holy Spirit to help us be trustworthy and honest. Even when it is difficult to be truthful, the Spirit of God can give us the strength and courage we need. The Holy Spirit can help us know how to do the right thing.

We need to remember to thank God for those who teach us about truth and honesty and for all the people whom we trust.

Activity

1. A girl from another country joined our class. Some of my friends make fun of her and say things about her that are untrue. I like my friends a lot. I do not want to lose them. With the help of the Holy Spirit,

   I could _____.

   I could _____.

2. Someone has been taking lunch money out of Ramón's desk. The teacher thinks that it's Ben. I know that it's really Marty who takes the money. With the help of the Holy Spirit,

   I could _____.

   I could _____.

Praying with Honesty

We have already learned how important it is to be honest with ourselves and with one another. But how honest are we with God? Circle the prayer below that you think is the most honest.

Bridget: "God, it's okay with me if I never get chosen to be a teacher's helper. I don't really want that job anyway."

Doug: "God, I just don't like Manuel. I don't want to feel this way but I just can't seem to help it. Why are some people so easy to like and others so difficult? Help me, Lord, to find something likable about Manuel."

Christine: "God, you know how much I love my family. I don't really mind that my brother teases me all the time or that my sister borrows my favorite sweater without asking permission."

Catholics believe that God knows us better than we know ourselves. There is no point being less than honest with God. Instead, we should be happy that the Lord knows us so well and loves us so much that we can always tell God what we are *really* feeling and thinking. We never have to hide anything from the One who created us.

Take some time to pray an honest prayer in the quiet of your heart.

Chapter Review

1. Think about a time when someone told a lie about you. What could you do so that you and that person could make peace with each other?

I could

_____

_____

2. We hurt others when we lie to them or about them. Think about a time when you may have hurt someone in this way. Write about what you will do to make up for the hurt.

I will

_____

_____

On the lines provided, write your answers to the first two questions.

1. What is meant by *bear false witness*?

_____

_____

2. Why should we respect the truth?

_____

_____

_____

_____

3. Discuss what the world would be like if no one followed the eighth commandment.

Speak the truth in love.
Based on Ephesians 4:15

15

Our Merciful God

When you have said or done wrong and hurtful things, what are some ways that you have been forgiven?

A Forgiving Mother

School ended early because of snow. Ellen invited Linda to go home with her. "Let's go to my house and do our homework together," Ellen suggested. "My mother is still at work."

Linda liked the idea, so the girls went to Ellen's house. Linda noticed a VCR and said, "Let's watch a movie instead of doing our homework. It looks like your mom has some good ones."

"We can't," Ellen answered. "My mother told me not to play any of her movies when she's not here."

"But your mother is at work," Linda said. "She'll never know."

Ellen thought for a minute, and then she shrugged her shoulders. "Okay," she agreed. "Let's watch a movie."

They were enjoying the movie when Ellen's mother unexpectedly came home an hour early.

"Ellen!" her mother said sternly. "Didn't I tell you not to play any movies when I'm not with you? Now go to your room! And Linda, I think you should go home."

Linda left quickly, and Ellen ran to her room, crying.

Ellen's mother hung up her coat, and then she went upstairs to speak to Ellen.

"I'm sorry, Ellen, but you shouldn't have touched the VCR and my movies when I had told you not to," she said.

Ellen put her arms around her mother. "I'm sorry," Ellen said. "I know I was wrong. But we didn't have much homework, and Linda wanted to watch a movie."

"Let's go downstairs and make dinner," Ellen's mother said. "Then maybe we can watch a movie together."

God Is a Forgiving Father

Even when we are very young, we make mistakes. As we grow older, we may choose to do wrong. But no matter how many times we choose to do wrong, our parents will always love us and forgive us.

God is a merciful father. The Lord always loves us and is eager to show us mercy. Like a loving father, God is ready to forgive us when we show that we are sorry. Our sorrow for sin and God's forgiveness lead to **reconciliation**.

Vocabulary

reconciliation: making up through sorrow and forgiveness

✦ ✦ ✦ ✦ ✦ ✦ ✦ ✦ ✦ ✦ ✦

We Believe

God the Father is merciful and forgiving. God keeps on loving us when we sin. The Lord is always ready to forgive us when we show that we are sorry.

In the following Scripture story, we learn that when people forgive each other they are imitating God, who is always ready to forgive. We also learn that we will be forgiven by God every time we ask.

A Merciful Father

One day, Jesus told this story about a merciful father. A man had two sons. One day his younger son came to him. "Father," the young man said, "please give me my share of the **inheritance**."

The father gave him his share. The younger son gathered up his belongings and left home to start a new life in a foreign country. There he lived a wild life and wasted all his money, until he had nothing left.

So the young man went to work for a farmer. The farmer put him to work caring for the pigs. The young man worked hard but did not make much money. Sometimes he was so hungry that he wanted to eat the pigs' food. Finally, the young man thought about his home. "Even my father's servants have enough to eat," he thought to himself, "and here I am starving. I'll go back to my father and tell him that I'm sorry. I do not deserve to be his son. I'll ask my father to take me back as one of his servants."

The next morning the young man set out for home. He was down the road from his father's house when his father saw him. His father's heart was filled with love and forgiveness. The father ran down the road to meet his son. He hugged and kissed him.

The young man began to say that he was sorry. "Father, I have sinned against God and against you. I no longer deserve to be your son."

But the father stopped him. He called to his servants, "Hurry! Bring my son some clean clothes. Put a ring on his finger and shoes on his feet. And prepare a grand celebration. My son, who was lost, is now found." Then the father took his son into the house.

Based on Luke 15:11–24

Discuss

Why do you think the young man thought he did not deserve to be treated as a son when he returned home?

Jesus Teaches About Reconciliation

The story that Jesus told about a son who is sorry and a father who forgives is really a story about God and us. We are like the son. When we sin and are sorry for our sins, we can ask the Father's forgiveness.

God is like the father in the Scripture story. God loves us no matter what we do and is eager to show us mercy. Like a loving father, God always forgives us when we are sorry for our sins.

We imitate God when we forgive people who hurt us, just as the father in the Scripture story forgave his son. We experience the Lord's forgiveness through people who forgive us.

Vocabulary

inheritance: the money and property received from someone who has died

◆ ◆ ◆ ◆ ◆ ◆ ◆ ◆ ◆ ◆ ◆ ◆

Maria's Birthday Present

Ever since she was in the second grade, Maria had wanted a pair of in-line skates. So, for her tenth birthday, Maria's parents took her shopping to buy the long-desired skates and the necessary safety equipment.

On the way home, Maria's parents made it clear: No skating in the street! EVER!

"Oh, no!" Maria promised, "I will never, never go in the street."

Day after day, Maria practiced on the sidewalk in front of her house. Every day she was getting more skilled in learning how to go faster and how to stop suddenly.

One day, as Maria was zipping down the sidewalk, instead of stopping where the sidewalk ended, she continued on the street. She looked at the wide street in front of her. This was really going to be exciting!

She was proud of how skillfully she skated down the hill. Suddenly, there was a car in front of her! The driver skidded to a screeching stop, leaving long black marks on the street. Maria glided on past the car, her heart pounding like a hammer.

It was a long time before Maria finally worked up her courage and headed for home. She knew that her parents would already know of the dangerously close call she had just had. After all, the driver of the car was their next door neighbor.

The Way to Forgiveness

When we want forgiveness, three things are necessary.

1. We must be sincerely sorry for what we have done.

2. We must say that we are sorry and ask forgiveness.

3. We must make a firm decision never to do it again.

We make these three promises to ourselves and to the person who forgives us. The promises are necessary when we ask forgiveness from God as well.

Activity

On the lines below, finish the story about Maria and her in-line skates. Tell what happened when she went into the house. Tell about Maria's need for forgiveness and reconciliation.

_____

_____

_____

_____

_____

_____

_____

_____

Continue reading the story that Jesus told about the merciful father.

A Merciful Father *(continued from pages 184, 185)*

While the father had been greeting his returning son, the older son was still out working in the field. As he was returning home from his day's labor, he heard the sounds of a party. He called to one of the servants and asked the reason for the party.

The servant answered, "Your brother has returned home. Your father is so happy that he is having a great feast."

The older son grew angry when he heard this and he would not join the festivities. But his father came out and began to plead with him.

The son said to his father, "For years I have stayed and worked for you. I never disobeyed one of your orders. Yet you never even let me have a party for my friends. Now, when my brother returns after wasting your money, you welcome him home with a celebration."

"My son," replied the father, "you are with me always. Everything I have is yours. But we have to celebrate and rejoice! Your brother was lost and now he is found."

Based on Luke 15:25–32

Called to Forgive Others

Just as God is merciful with us, we must be merciful with one another. In the Scripture story, "A Merciful Father," it wasn't enough for the father to forgive his son and welcome him home. The boy's father urged the older son to do the same.

We are like the older son. Jesus calls us to forgive our brothers and sisters, neighbors, friends, parents, and any one else who asks our forgiveness.

Even though it is often difficult to forgive others, many people in our lives give us wonderful examples. Each time our families forgive us, they show us how to forgive. Each time our friends and classmates are merciful with us, we learn how to be merciful with others.

Jesus is our greatest teacher of mercy and forgiveness. In many gospel stories, we can read about Jesus forgiving others. Even as Jesus was dying on the cross, he forgave the people who put him there.

Activity

Read the story below. Then on the lines below the story, write the advice you would offer to each person.

Jessica was very helpful at home last week. But Dad asked Jessica's brother to go to the soccer game instead of inviting her. Jessica stormed up the steps and slammed the door of her bedroom when she found out.

Dad looked at Joe and asked, "What should we do now?" Joe didn't know what to say.

My advice to Jessica is _____.

My advice to Jessica's dad is _____.

My advice to Joe is _____.

Praying a Prayer of Mercy

Kyrie Eleison is a prayer that we often pray at Mass. The Greek words *Kyrie eleison* mean, "Lord, have mercy." For hundreds of years, the Church used the Greek words to pray this prayer. Now it is usually prayed in the language of the people. Kyrie Eleison is a prayer praising the Lord's great kindness and merciful love.

Teacher: Let us pray.

All: In the name of the Father, and of the Son, and of the Holy Spirit. Amen.

Teacher: Let us ask the Lord's mercy on us all. Kyrie eleison.

Students: Kyrie eleison. Lord, have mercy.

Teacher: Christe eleison.

Students: Christe eleison. Christ, have mercy.

Teacher: Kyrie eleison.

Students Kyrie eleison. Lord, have mercy.

Teacher: Let us pray together a psalm in praise of God's mercy.

All: The Lord is merciful and loving,
slow to become angry and full of kindness.
As high as the sky is above the earth,
so great is God's love for those who love the Lord.
As far as the east is from the west,
so far does God put our sins from us.
As a father understands his children,
so God understands those who honor the Lord.

Based on Psalm 103:8–13

Chapter Review

Name three things that are necessary
for forgiveness.

1. _____

2. _____

3. _____

In this chapter you have read three stories
about forgiveness and reconciliation. Fill in
the blanks to complete the sentences.

1. _____ teaches us about
reconciliation in the Scripture story about
a merciful father.

2. _____ is always willing to forgive
us. We can learn how to be forgiving

people by following our _____
example when they forgive us.

On the lines provided, write your answers to the
first two questions.

1. What is meant by *reconciliation*?

_____

_____

2. When does God forgive us?

_____

_____

_____

3. Discuss ways that people experience God's
mercy and forgiveness.

**The Lord is kind
and merciful. God
forgives our sins.**
Based on Sirach 2:11

Bringing God's Forgiveness

Think of a time when someone forgave you. Describe how you felt before you were forgiven and how you felt afterward.

Activity

The picture story is about Jake and Melissa. On the lines below, tell how you think the story should end.

_____

_____

_____

_____

_____

_____

Jesus Forgives His Friend

The enemies of Jesus had taken him to the home of the high priest. Jesus was questioned there. While this was going on, Jesus' enemies waited outside.

It was a cool night so they lit a fire in the yard to keep warm. One of Jesus' disciples, Peter, sat with them. He was afraid. Peter hoped that no one would remember that he was a friend of Jesus.

A servant girl noticed Peter. She stared at him for a while. Then she pointed to Peter and said, "This man was with Jesus."

"You're wrong," Peter answered. "I don't even know Jesus."

A few minutes later a man looked carefully at Peter. "You are one of Jesus' friends," he said.

Peter answered, "No, I am not one of them."

About an hour later another person was sure that Peter was one of Jesus' friends. "This man was certainly with Jesus, for he is a **Galilean**," the person said to those around the fire.

Again Peter said, "Woman, I don't know what you are talking about."

Just then soldiers led Jesus out of the high priest's house. Peter looked at Jesus. Jesus saw Peter and knew that Peter's heart was filled with sadness. Peter was sorry for what he had done. He knew that Jesus forgave him.

Peter ran out of the yard. He sat down beside the road and cried for a long time.

Based on Luke 22:54–62

Vocabulary

Galilean: someone from Galilee, the land north of Samaria

◆ ◆ ◆ ◆ ◆ ◆ ◆ ◆ ◆ ◆ ◆

Activity

Complete the following sentences with ideas of your own.

1. To be a good parent, a person needs to be _____.

2. To be a good son or daughter, a person needs to be _____.

3. To be a good Christian, a person needs to be _____.

Jesus Brings God's Forgiveness

In the Scripture story about Peter and Jesus found on page 193, Jesus forgave Peter. Peter cried not only because he was sorry for what he had done but also because he felt Jesus' forgiveness.

Jesus spent much of his life bringing God's mercy to people who had sinned. The gospels tell us that Jesus went from town to town, looking for people who needed human **compassion** and God's forgiveness. Jesus forgave people whom the Temple priests said could not be forgiven, even by God.

Jesus forgave Judas, who had betrayed him. Even as Jesus hung on the cross, he asked God to forgive those who were responsible for his death.

When looking up a Scripture passage, follow these steps.

Example: **Matthew 9:35-37**

STEP 1: **Matthew**   Find *The Gospel According to Matthew*, located in the second half of the Bible.

STEP 2: **9**   Look at the tops of the pages and find *Matthew 9*. This means Matthew's Gospel, Chapter 9. Look at the pages of Matthew 9 to find the beginning of the chapter.

STEP 3: **35–37**   Notice that the first sentence in Chapter 9 has been marked with a small **1**. Scan the story until you find a small verse **35**. Now read verses 35–37.

Activity

Using a Bible, locate the following gospel stories that give examples of how Jesus showed compassion for others. Then, on the lines provided, tell who received Jesus' loving compassion.

Matthew 20: 29–34

_____

Mark 1: 40–41

_____

Luke 15: 11–32

_____

Vocabulary

compassion: feeling another's pain and wanting to relieve it

✦ ✦ ✦ ✦ ✦ ✦ ✦ ✦ ✦ ✦

We Believe

Jesus came to bring God's mercy to everyone. He continues to bring God's forgiveness to those who show that they are sorry for their sins.

Jesus Teaches About Forgiveness

As Jesus went about Galilee preaching, he often taught about forgiveness. We read in the Bible about the many times Jesus taught about forgiveness by his example. We have just read about Jesus forgiving Peter. We know that even as Jesus was dying on the cross, he forgave those who crucified him. We know the story of Zacchaeus. Jesus brought God's mercy through his example and his teaching.

As the people and the disciples saw these examples of forgiveness, many began to ask Jesus what was expected of them. In the Gospel of Matthew we read about one of the times Jesus taught about forgiveness with words rather than by example.

Peter came up to Jesus and asked him this question. "Lord, when my brother does something against me, how often must I forgive him? Seven times?"

"No," Jesus replied, "not seven times. I say seventy times seven times."

Based on Matthew 18:21–22

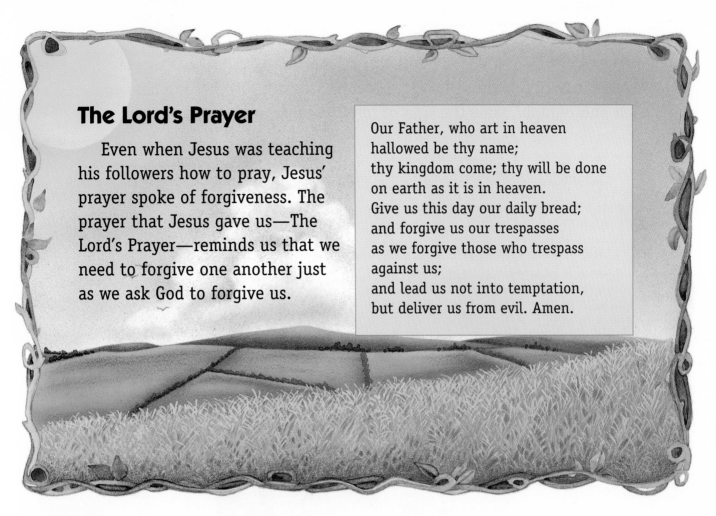

The Lord's Prayer

Even when Jesus was teaching his followers how to pray, Jesus' prayer spoke of forgiveness. The prayer that Jesus gave us—The Lord's Prayer—reminds us that we need to forgive one another just as we ask God to forgive us.

Our Father, who art in heaven
hallowed be thy name;
thy kingdom come; thy will be done
on earth as it is in heaven.
Give us this day our daily bread;
and forgive us our trespasses
as we forgive those who trespass
against us;
and lead us not into temptation,
but deliver us from evil. Amen.

Activity

Prayerfully read and think about the meaning of The Lord's Prayer. Then write the answers to the following questions.

1. With which words of the prayer do we bless God's name?

_____

2. With which words of the prayer do we ask God's forgiveness?

_____

3. Which words express our promise to God that we will be forgiving?

_____

4. With which words do we ask God to keep us from the temptations and evils in the world?

_____

_____

Activity

Words are only one sign that expresses forgiveness. On the line next to each photograph, name the sign of forgiveness being offered.

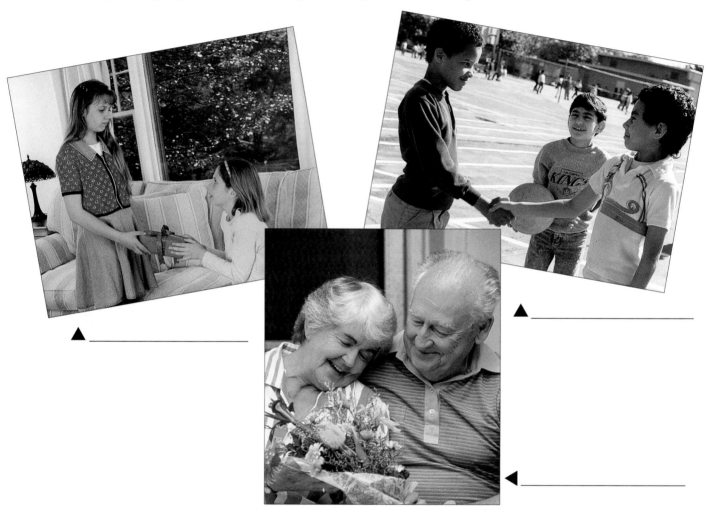

▲ _____

▲ _____

◀ _____

Forgiveness Through the Sacraments

God invites us to be forgiven and to be forgiving people. God's forgiveness comes to us through the many ways people forgive each other. Catholics believe that Jesus also brings us God's forgiveness through the Church's sacraments.

In the sacrament of Baptism we become a part of a people who are both forgiven and forgiving. Through Baptism, original sin and all other sins are forgiven.

In the sacrament of the Eucharist, we share in the peace that Jesus won for us by his death and resurrection. The Church teaches that the Eucharist is an important source of reconciliation.

In the sacrament of Reconciliation, we celebrate forgiveness and peace. When we celebrate this sacrament, we celebrate God's faithful mercy and forgiveness.

When we are sick, the sacrament of Anointing of the Sick brings us Jesus' forgiveness, healing, and peace.

Activity

The photographs below show the four sacraments through which Jesus brings us God's forgiveness. Write the names of the sacraments shown to complete the sentences.

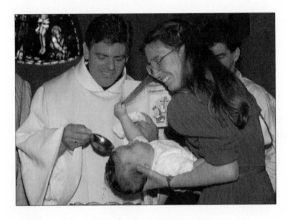

1. Jesus forgives through

_____.

2. Jesus forgives through

_____.

3. Jesus forgives through

_____.

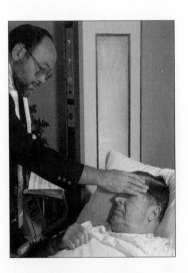

4. Jesus forgives through

_____.

Praying the Eucharistic Prayer

The Eucharistic Prayer is the great prayer of thanks prayed at Mass during the Liturgy of the Eucharist. In this prayer the priest thanks God for all the gifts of creation and especially for God's greatest gift, Jesus.

During the Eucharistic Prayer, we remember Jesus' sacrifice on the cross. We hear the priest pray the same words that Jesus used at the Last Supper.

At the end of the Eucharistic Prayer, we join the priest in praying together the Great Amen. Our Amen says that we add our consent to the great prayer of thanks the priest just prayed. We are indeed grateful for all God's gifts to us, especially Jesus.

Join your teacher and classmates in praying the following prayer, taken from the Eucharistic Prayer for Masses with Children II.

All: Blessed be Jesus, whom you sent
to be the friend of children and of the poor.

Teacher: He came to show us
how we can love you, Father,
by loving one another.
He came to take away sin,
which keeps us from being friends,
and hate, which makes us all unhappy.

He promised to send the Holy Spirit
to be with us always
so that we can live as your children.

All: Blessed is he who comes in the name of the Lord.
Hosanna in the highest.

Chapter Review

Place the words in the box below into the correct sentences.

Judas	Peter	Baptism	Reconciliation	peace

1. Jesus forgave ———— when he said he didn't know Jesus.

2. Jesus forgave ———— even after he betrayed Jesus.

3. The sacrament of ———— forgives original sin and all other sins..

4. The sacrament of ———— celebrates God's faithful mercy and forgiveness.

5. In the sacrament of the Eucharist, we share in the ———— Jesus won for us.

Write your answers to the first two questions on the lines provided.

1. What is meant by *compassion*?

_____

_____

2. How does Jesus bring God's forgiveness to people today?

_____

_____

_____

Forgive as the Lord forgives you.
Colossians 3:13

3. Discuss how we can act like Jesus and be forgiving.

UNIT 4 ORGANIZER

Chapter 13: Respecting What Belongs to Others

Chapter 14: Respecting the Truth

Summarize the main ideas of each chapter in this unit.

Chapter 15: Our Merciful God

Chapter 16: Bringing God's Forgiveness

UNIT 4 REVIEW

Read each statement below. Then write **True** or **False** on the line in front of each statement.

1. _____ Greed is wanting more and more things when they are not needed.

2. _____ Cheating is one way of showing love for our neighbor.

3. _____ When we lie, we bear false witness.

4. _____ Reconciliation is making up through sorrow and forgiveness.

5. _____ Envy is wanting something that belongs to another person.

6. _____ Sometimes lying doesn't hurt anyone.

Each statement describes an action that shows we are following a certain commandment. Write the number of that commandment in the blank next to the statement.

1. _____ We do not take from others what belongs to them.

2. _____ We fight against feelings of envy in our hearts.

3. _____ We respect the truth.

4. _____ We share what we have with others.

5. _____ We do not cause deliberate harm to another's property.

6. _____ We are not careless or wasteful.

7. _____ We do not spread rumors or gossip about others.

8. _____ We give thanks for all that God has given us.

UNIT 4 REVIEW

Circle the letter of the word needed to complete each sentence correctly.

1. God is always ready to _____ us when we show that we are sorry.

   (a) punish   **(b)** forgive   **(c)** forget

2. In the story of the merciful father, we are like the _____.

   (a) servants   **(b)** father   **(c)** lost son

3. Jesus came to bring God's forgiveness to _____.

   (a) everyone   **(b)** saints   **(c)** Peter

4. When we lie, we hurt _____.

   (a) ourselves   **(b)** others   **(c)** ourselves and others

5. In reconciliation, we make up through _____.

   (a) forgiveness   **(b)** sorrow   **(c)** sorrow and forgiveness

6. Jesus taught that we must forgive each other _____ times.

   (a) 7   **(b)** 70   **(c)** 70 times 7

Finish the sentences below by giving one example of a sin against the commandment.

1. We sin against the seventh commandment when we

_____

2. We sin against the eighth commandment when we

_____

3. We sin against the tenth commandment when we

_____

WHEN SAYING YES SOMETIMES MEANS SAYING NO

By choosing to do what we know is right we say yes to Jesus' call to be his followers. Sometimes doing the right thing can be an unpopular choice. It may mean saying no to what our friends want us to do. We may experience doubt about our choice and worry that others might think we aren't cool. Doing the loving thing isn't always the popular thing to do. Sometimes being a follower of Jesus means risking others' disapproval.

What Should David Do?

David and two of his friends walk home from school together every day. They usually stop at the convenience store for a soft drink. Lately David's friends have been sneaking candy bars out of the store in their pockets. This has gone on for a week or two, and now they are pressuring David to do the same. They tell David that taking the candy is no big deal. The candy costs less than a dollar, and besides, it's the store owners' fault for not watching their customers. They call David "chicken".

How do you think David is feeling?

What do his friends want him to do?

What do you think David wants to do?

What do you think is the right thing for David to do?

What choice does David need to make to show that he is a follower of Jesus?

Let's suppose that David believes that stealing is wrong and chooses not to steal the candy. His friends continue to pressure him. They call him names and make fun of him. Even when they are away from the store, his friends still taunt him. David feels angry and hurt by their behavior.

David is unsure about what to do. David is tempted to strike out at his friends, yet he knows that fighting is a hurtful response and goes against what it means to be a follower of Jesus.

Can you think of some things David might do to help himself feel better without hurting someone else? List your ideas on the lines below.

_____

_____

_____

One of the things David decides to do is to tell his friends how he feels about their teasing. When telling how he feels, David needs to remember to

- use "I"-language. Begin by saying "I feel_____,

  when you _____"

- use a firm voice tone.

- look at the other person when speaking to them. This is called eye contact.

- stand tall. Lean your body slightly toward the other person.

Following Jesus

Just like David, we are involved in lots of different situations where we have to make decisions about how we are going to act. The choices we make can lead us closer to Jesus and the type of persons he calls us to be as his followers, or can move us farther away.

PRAYER

Jesus, wrap your love around me. Help me share your love through my words and actions. Help me follow you even when the path is difficult. Amen.

OPENING DOORS

A Take-Home Magazine™

Growing Closer

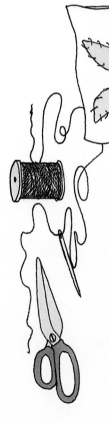

MAKE A FAMILY PEACE QUILT. Use large patches of felt as the background. Use pieces of brightly colored felt for each family member to cut out designs for his or her patch.

Then use heavy thread or yarn to sew the pieces together. Through the years, you may wish to add patches to the quilt. Keep the quilt in your living room as a sign of family unity and peace.

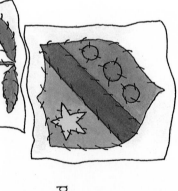

Looking Ahead

Unit 5 looks at how the Church helps us celebrate God's forgiveness in the sacrament of Reconciliation, build community in Eucharist, and become shining examples of goodness and service to the world. Your fourth grader will come to realize that people should be able to look at any parish community and recognize the attitudes and actions of Jesus Christ.

8

UNMASKING PROBLEMS

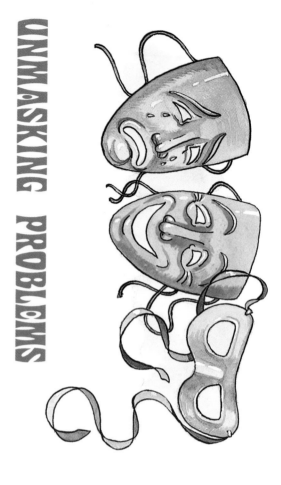

The rapid rate of growth and maturation in your child may lead you to forget how fragile his or her feelings may be. You may not always be able to read your child's faces, moods, verbal or nonverbal responses to your questions, corrections, or statements.

As your child continues to mature, each choice or decision he or she makes holds more facets. And even though your child may send out messages of independence, he or she still wants clear and consistent adult direction and honesty.

When there are problems or conflicts of family life, masks of indifference or escape may be worn. To prevent this from happening, invite your child to participate with the entire family in problem solving. You may find the conflict-resolution process on page 3 helpful.

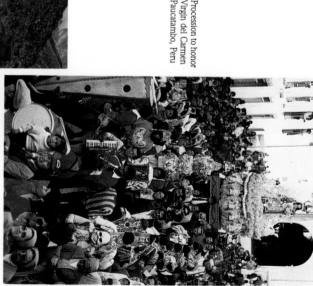

A musical procession
Qoyllur Rit'i
Cusco, Peru

Procession to honor
Virgin del Carmen
Paucatambo, Peru

Pilgrimage to the Virgin
of Copacabana, Bolivia

FACING THE ISSUES

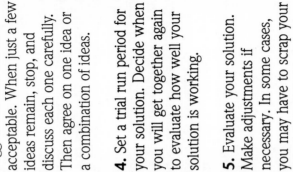

1. State the problem or conflict clearly. Sometimes you may have to weed out side issues to discover the main problem.

2. Brainstorm possible solutions to the problem. List everyone's suggestions even though you think some are far-fetched.

3. Take turns crossing off suggestions that are not acceptable. When just a few ideas remain, stop, and discuss each one carefully. Then agree on one idea or a combination of ideas.

4. Set a trial run period for your solution. Decide when you will get together again to evaluate how well your solution is working.

5. Evaluate your solution. Make adjustments if necessary. In some cases, you may have to scrap your solution because it is not working at all. You may agree then to try another idea that was first rejected.

Mary, a Sign of Hope

Nativity. Serigraph. Sadao Watanabe, Japan, 1970.

. . . Mary shines forth on earth, until the day of the Lord shall come as a sign of sure hope and solace for the pilgrim People of God.
(Dogmatic Constitution on the Church No. 68)

Facing Our Humanity

The most basic kind of honesty is being honest with ourselves before God. To help you understand this truth, Jesus told the following parable.

"Two people went up to the temple area to pray; one was a Pharisee and the other was a tax collector. The Pharisee took up his position and spoke this prayer to himself, 'O God, I thank you that I am not like the rest of humanity—greedy, dishonest, adulterous—or even like this tax collector. I fast twice a week, and I pay tithes on my whole income.' But the tax collector stood off at a distance and would not even raise his eyes to heaven but beat his breast and prayed, 'O God, be merciful to me a sinner.' I tell you, the latter went home justified, not the former."

Luke 18:10-14

During the Penitential Rite at Mass, we each have a chance to turn to God and admit our failures and sins. The priest invites us to do this in one of the following ways.

As we prepare to celebrate the mystery of Christ's love, let us acknowledge our failures and ask the Lord for pardon and strength.

Coming together as God's family, with confidence let us ask the Father's forgiveness, for he is full of gentleness and compassion.

My brothers and sisters, to prepare ourselves to celebrate the sacred mysteries, let us call to mind our sins.

We respond by honestly admitting that we have failed and confidently ask for God's mercy and forgiveness.

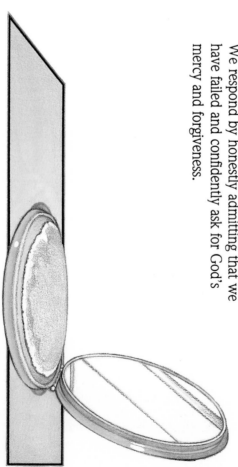

UNIT 5

Celebrating and Serving

What can we do to make the world a better place?

17

The Sacrament of Reconciliation

What are some things you have done to make up with someone you have wronged or hurt?

The Missing Pieces

"I have a board game that I'm tired of," Becky told her best friend, Kate. "And you have two trivia games. I'll trade you my board game for one of your trivia games."

"Okay," Kate agreed. "That's a fair trade."

Becky was happy to be rid of her board game because she knew that it was missing some pieces.

That night, Kate and her grandfather decided to play the board game. After a few minutes, they realized that some of the pieces were missing. Kate was angry.

The next morning, Kate went to Becky's house. "Give back my trivia game, you cheater!" Kate shouted. "You knew there were pieces missing from the board game."

For three weeks the two friends did not talk to each other. Then one Saturday morning, Becky's mother asked her daughter, "What's wrong between you and Kate?"

"We're mad at each other," Becky said. "Kate thinks I knew that the board game I traded for her trivia game was missing some pieces."

"Did you?" Becky's mother asked. When Becky did not answer, her mother said, "Becky, if you did try to cheat your friend, you need to tell Kate you are sorry. If she forgives you, then you can be friends again."

Becky thought about what her mother had said. The next day she went to Kate's house. "Kate," Becky said, "it's my fault. I did try to cheat you, and I'm sorry. I would really like to be your friend again."

"It's okay," Kate answered.

"I'll give back your trivia game," Becky promised. "Let's do something special to celebrate making up and being friends again."

Being Reconciled

Sometimes we hurt others. Then often we are sorry and want to be forgiven. We want to be reconciled. When this happens, we need to go to the person we have hurt and admit that we have done something wrong. We need to ask forgiveness.

We are unhappy when we are separated from one another. When we forgive and make up, we celebrate because we are happy to be united and forgiven.

Catholics have a very special way of celebrating God's forgiveness and expressing sorrow for sins. We call this sacramental celebration *Reconciliation* or *Penance.*

Recognizing Our Sins

We know that God is always ready to forgive us. Because God is merciful, we can honestly admit our sins and express our sorrow. But how can we recognize our sins?

Sometimes our families or teachers tell us when we have done something wrong. They can help us know right from wrong.

At other times we know that we have done something wrong by the way we feel. We feel guilty about what we have done. We hope that nobody finds out about it. We may even be afraid that we will be punished.

When we experience these feelings, our conscience is helping us recognize that we have sinned. Our conscience is our power to judge between good and evil.

At these times we can think about Jesus' Great Commandment, the Beatitudes, and the Ten Commandments. We can ask ourselves if we have been following these laws. When we ask ourselves these questions, we are making an **examination of conscience.**

Activity

Read these questions and think about each one. What are some other questions you can ask yourself? Write those questions on the lines provided.

My Love for God

- Do I use God's name respectfully?
- Do I pray? Do I worship God on Sunday?

_____

_____

My Love for Myself

- Do I care for my health?
- Do I improve my talents by study and practice?
- Do I respect my body?

_____

_____

My Love for Others

- Do I treat others fairly and with respect?
- Do I obey my parents and those responsible for me?
- Do I tell the truth?
- Do I respect others' bodies and belongings?

_____

_____

My Love for the World

- Do I use things with care? Do I respect the environment?
- Do I respect things that belong to others?
- Do I share what I have with those who have less?

_____

_____

Vocabulary

examination of conscience: thinking about what we have said and done and how we may have sinned

✖ ✖ ✖ ✖ ✖ ✖ ✖ ✖ ✖ ✖ ✖ ✖

The Sacrament of Reconciliation ~~~

Sometimes we do not live lovingly and responsibly, as Jesus wants us to live. We sin, but we want to make up for our sin. We celebrate God's forgiveness in the sacrament of Reconciliation.

There are two ways we normally celebrate this sacrament. One way is together as a community. This is called *communal* reconciliation. When we celebrate the sacrament without the community gathered, it is called *individual* reconciliation.

In both ways of celebrating reconciliation, we need to pray and make an examination of conscience before going to the priest to confess our sins. We think about how we have lived since our last celebration of this sacrament. We think about any sins we may have committed. Then we go to the priest and do four important things.

Individual Reconciliation

When we celebrate this sacrament we do four important things.

1. We confess our sins to the priest.

We go to the priest in the reconciliation room. We can sit in a chair, facing the priest, or we can kneel behind a screen that separates the priest from us.

2. We accept a penance.

The priest talks to us about our sins and gives us a penance. The penance can be a prayer that we pray or a task that we do, such as helping the poor. Doing the penance will help us avoid sinning in the future.

3. We express our sorrow.

We tell God and the priest that we are sorry for our sins. We ask forgiveness. We can use our own words, or we can pray an act of contrition, a prayer of sorrow.

4. We receive **absolution** from the priest.

The priest stretches out his hands over us. He prays the words of absolution. He asks God to forgive our sins. Jesus acts through the Church to bring us God's forgiveness. When the priest absolves us, the risen Christ absolves us.

Communal Reconciliation

When a group of Catholics celebrates this sacrament together, it is called communal reconciliation. Several priests are present. Usually there are Scripture readings, songs, and prayers. In the communal celebration a priest leads everyone through the sacrament together. But the confession of sins, the acceptance of a penance, and the receiving of the priest's absolution are still done individually.

Vocabulary

absolution: the prayer of forgiveness prayed by the priest in the sacrament of Reconciliation

✖ ✖ ✖ ✖ ✖ ✖ ✖ ✖ ✖ ✖ ✖ ✖

We Believe

In the sacrament of Reconciliation, the Church celebrates God's forgiveness.

The Lost Sheep

One day, Jesus told his friends this parable:

"There once was a shepherd who had one hundred sheep. One day the shepherd noticed that one of the sheep had wandered away. The shepherd loved his sheep and was very upset to have lost even one of them.

"The shepherd decided that he must leave the ninety-nine sheep grazing on the mountainside and go in search of the lost sheep. And when he found his lost sheep, he picked up the sheep and carried it home on his shoulders, rejoicing.

"So it is with God. There is greater rejoicing and celebrating in heaven over one sinner who returns and asks forgiveness than over ninety-nine persons who have no need of forgiveness."

Based on Luke 15: 1–7

Discuss

1. Why was the shepherd so worried about losing one of his sheep when he still had ninety-nine others?

2. If you were the shepherd, would you do what the shepherd in this Scripture story did? Why or why not?

Celebrating God's Forgiveness

The sacrament of Reconciliation gives us many reasons to rejoice and celebrate. We celebrate because the sacrament gives us an opportunity to admit our sins, ask forgiveness, and experience reconciliation with God and with those we've hurt. We know that God has forgiven us and has taken away all our guilt. We are no longer separated from one another. Instead, we are friends, once more united in peace and love. We can begin again to follow Jesus more closely and faithfully.

Activity

Put a ✔ in front of the occasions listed below in which forgiveness and reconciliation were a real celebration in your life.

_____ After a family argument

_____ After a fight with a friend

_____ After celebrating the sacrament of Reconciliation

_____ After saying hurtful words to a classmate

_____ After having a serious talk with a parent

_____ After getting in trouble in school

_____ Other _____

Praying an Act of Contrition

The Act of Contrition is a special prayer that allows us to tell God that we are sorry for our sins. The word *contrition* means "sincere sorrow." When we pray this prayer, we are expressing sincere sorrow for our sins.

A prayer of contrition is often prayed as part of our celebration of the sacrament of Reconciliation. It can also be prayed when we examine our conscience before celebrating the sacrament.

As we get ready for bed each night, it is good for us to recall our words and actions of the day. It can also be a time for us to pray a prayer of contrition. Memorize the Act of Contrition below or another prayer of sorrow used in your school or parish.

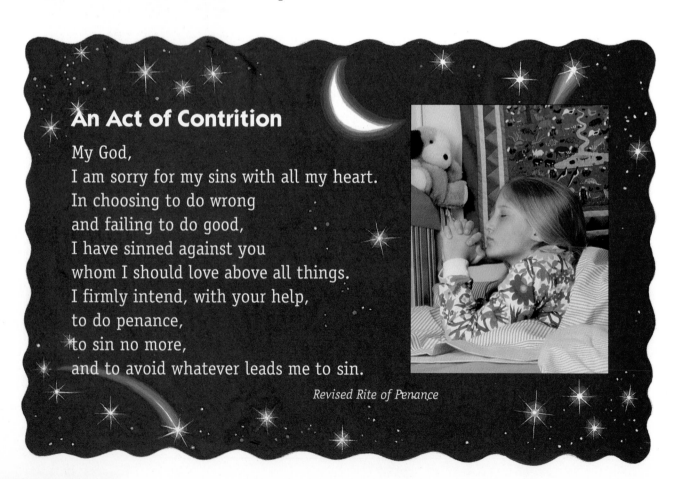

An Act of Contrition

My God,
I am sorry for my sins with all my heart.
In choosing to do wrong
and failing to do good,
I have sinned against you
whom I should love above all things.
I firmly intend, with your help,
to do penance,
to sin no more,
and to avoid whatever leads me to sin.

Revised Rite of Penance

Chapter Review

What are the four steps of the sacrament of Reconciliation?

1. _____

2. _____

3. _____

4. _____

In what two ways can we celebrate the sacrament?

1. _____

2. _____

1. Why is there a sacrament of Reconciliation?

_____

_____

_____

_____

_____

2. What is an examination of conscience?

_____

_____

_____

_____

3. Discuss how we can be reconcilers, helping people make up through sorrow and forgiveness.

Through our Lord Jesus Christ, we have received reconciliation with God.
Based on
Romans 5:11

Unity Through the Eucharist

18

What are some things that are more fun to do with others rather than alone?

Around the Campfire

Mrs. Garcia's class went on a picnic. Mrs. Garcia watched as groups of children went off to play.

"Let's go and play tennis," she heard Jeff suggest.

"That's a good idea," Luke agreed. "Nobody can play tennis like us."

So Jeff, Luke, and two other friends found a place to play tennis.

About the same time, Lucy said to Denise, "Why don't we play volleyball?"

Denise liked the idea. She invited six other friends to join her and Lucy.

Vincent brought a soccer ball with him to the picnic. He and his friends were the best soccer players in the class. He called Mario. Mario called Doug. Doug called his sister, Gina. Then they went off to practice together.

Another group of children formed at one of the picnic tables. They were having a good time putting together a huge jigsaw puzzle.

Mrs. Garcia knew that it was good for the children to have different likes and talents. But she thought to herself, "After the children play their favorite games, we should eat together around the campfire. Then they will feel how good it is to be with all the others."

As evening came, Mrs. Garcia lit the campfire. Everyone gathered around it. There were large jugs of juice. The children filled their cups from the jugs. They all roasted their hot dogs over the campfire. They passed a tray of rolls around so that each child could take a roll.

Mrs. Garcia and the class laughed and talked together as they ate by the campfire. "This is great!" Juan said. "We are a terrific class!"

Discuss

1. Why did Mrs. Garcia want the children to come together for their meal?

2. Why do you think that eating together helps people feel closer to one another?

Christians Share in Community

Like the people in Mrs. Garcia's class, each person has special interests, gifts, and talents to bring to his or her school community. In the same way, each Catholic has special gifts to bring to the Catholic community we know as the Church. The **Catholic Church** is the Christian community which celebrates the seven sacraments and recognizes the pope and bishops as its leaders.

Vocabulary

Catholic Church: the Christian community which celebrates the seven sacraments and recognizes the pope and bishops as its leaders

✖ ✖ ✖ ✖ ✖ ✖ ✖ ✖ ✖ ✖ ✖ ✖

One Bread, One Body

After Jesus died and rose from the dead, he invited Paul to be an apostle. Paul learned to love Jesus and to follow his ways.

Paul became a great Christian leader. He was the first to tell the **Corinthians**, the people of Corinth, a city in Greece, about Jesus. He organized the Christian community there.

But after a time, the Corinthians broke up into a number of separate groups. Each group felt that the members of their group were better Christians than the members of the other groups.

Paul heard about how the groups had divided. He was very sad. He wrote a long letter to all the Christians in Corinth. He told them that differences were good but that all Christians should be united. He told them that the Eucharist is a source of unity and love. Part of Paul's letter to the Corinthians is on the next page.

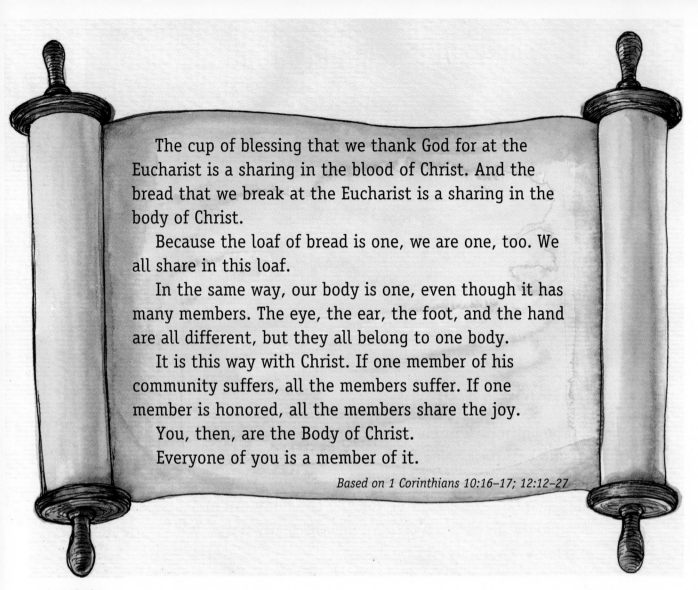

The cup of blessing that we thank God for at the Eucharist is a sharing in the blood of Christ. And the bread that we break at the Eucharist is a sharing in the body of Christ.

Because the loaf of bread is one, we are one, too. We all share in this loaf.

In the same way, our body is one, even though it has many members. The eye, the ear, the foot, and the hand are all different, but they all belong to one body.

It is this way with Christ. If one member of his community suffers, all the members suffer. If one member is honored, all the members share the joy.

You, then, are the Body of Christ.

Everyone of you is a member of it.

Based on 1 Corinthians 10:16–17; 12:12–27

Activity

1. Name one gift or talent that you share for the good of your class.

   _____

2. Name someone in your class who shares his or her gifts for the good of the whole class.

   _____

3. Name some ways your class shows that it is a community.

   _____

   _____

   _____

Vocabulary

Corinthians: The people who lived in Corinth, a city in Greece

✘ ✘ ✘ ✘ ✘ ✘ ✘ ✘ ✘ ✘ ✘ ✘

Unity in the Eucharist

The Catholic Church celebrates its unity at the Eucharist. Even though Catholics come from many different places and have many different gifts, in the Eucharist we are one. We eat and drink from the same table as a family. Sharing the body of Christ helps us to become the Body of Christ. We may be many parts, but we are all one body, the Body of Christ.

As Catholics we share special signs of our unity. The Church celebrates and deepens its unity at the Eucharist. We experience our unity through a variety of signs and actions.

1. As we gather to celebrate the Eucharist, we come together from many families and neighborhoods. We bring different gifts and the experiences of our lives. Still, we are one community that is gathered. We stand together. We sing together. We pray together. We are one family, the family of Jesus.

2. During the penitential rite, we ask forgiveness for any actions that may have separated us from one another and threatened our unity.

3. We tell the story of Jesus. As we hear the gospel proclaimed, we all stand as a sign of our respect for Jesus. The gospel message calls all Christians to unity.

4. We profess our faith. Together we say that we all believe in one God. We believe in God's only Son, Jesus. We share one faith. We are one because we all believe in Jesus and the Church.

5. We pray The Lord's Prayer together because it is the prayer given to us by Jesus and is prayed by all Christians. In some parishes, the people hold hands while they pray The Lord's Prayer as a physical sign of their unity.

6. We share the greeting of peace with one another as a reminder of our unity as brothers and sisters of Jesus.

7. We share a meal. As a family, we are all fed at the same table. As we share in the one body and blood of Jesus, we are strengthened in our unity with Jesus and with one another.

8. As the Mass ends, we are sent forth to live united as the Body of Christ in the world.

We Believe

The Church is called to be a community. We gather at the Eucharist to celebrate our unity and to help it grow.

Activity

The photographs below show some ways that people live in unity. Next to each photograph, write how the people are expressing their unity.

◀ _____

_____

_____

_____

_____ ▶

_____

_____

_____

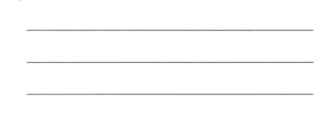

◀ _____

_____

_____

_____

Working for Unity

Living together in unity is not always easy. We have to work hard at being together in peace. To live in unity means that we learn to respect our differences and overlook each other's faults. We need to forgive one another and care about what is best for the entire Christian community.

It is easy to take one another for granted in our families. We must learn to appreciate the gifts of each family member. It may not be easy for everyone to live in harmony and unity, but we can work at it.

We have many different kinds of people in our classroom. We have different interests and talents. We have different ideas and opinions. Sometimes it is hard to agree, but we can work at it.

In our neighborhoods and towns, we have people of many different ages, ethnic backgrounds, and religions. We look different from one another, and we may even speak different languages. Although it may not always be easy to live in unity, we can work at it.

In all of these communities, our lives can show the unity that we celebrate in the Eucharist.

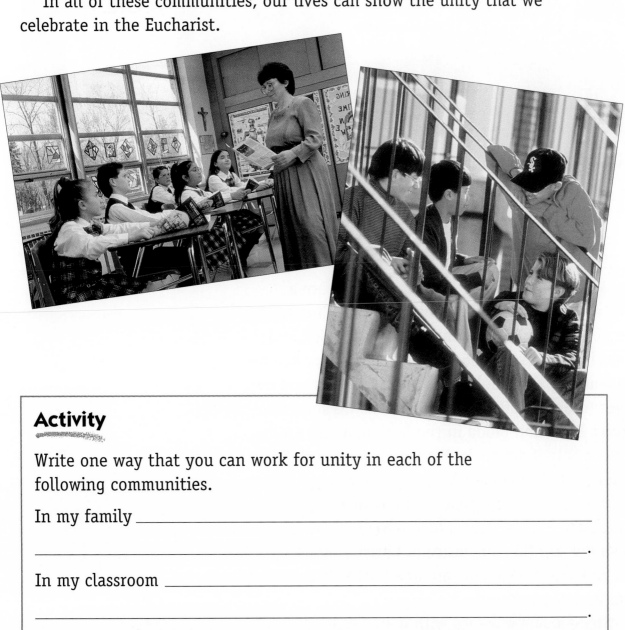

Activity

Write one way that you can work for unity in each of the following communities.

In my family _____

_____.

In my classroom _____

_____.

In my neighborhood _____

_____.

Praying a Sign of Peace and Unity

When we gather at the Eucharist, we are a united community of believers in Jesus Christ. As one body, the Body of Christ, we praise God and hear his word proclaimed in the Scriptures. As one community of Catholics, we offer our gifts and our lives to God in praise. We are one as we share in Jesus' Body and Blood in the Eucharist. We are no longer only individuals. We are now a united community of people who believe in Jesus.

One sign of unity that we share at Mass is called the Sign of Peace. At the Sign of Peace, we wish one another the peace of Christ and are reminded again that we are one family of believers, united in Jesus.

Share a sign of peace with your teacher and classmates.

Chapter Review

Eight signs of unity that we share in the Eucharist are listed below, but not in the correct order. Put them in the correct order by numbering them as they happen at Mass.

_____ We are sent forth.

_____ We profess our faith.

_____ We share a meal.

_____ We gather.

_____ We tell the story of Jesus.

_____ We ask forgiveness.

_____ We pray The Lord's Prayer.

_____ We share the greeting of peace.

1. Who were the Corinthians?

   _____

   _____

2. What does the Church celebrate at the Eucharist?

   _____

   _____

   _____

   _____

All who eat the bread of life are one.
Based on
1 Corinthians 10:17

3. Discuss what we can do to help build unity in the groups we belong to.

A Light to the World

What images and feelings does the word *light* suggest?

Activity

Imagine that you are each of the following sources of light. Complete the sentences below by writing ways each source of light helps people. Then name your own light source and complete the related sentence.

I am the sun. My light

_____

_____.

I am a neon light. My light

_____

_____.

I am _____. My light

_____

_____.

Shining Examples

Light helps us in many ways. It helps us when we cannot find our way, and it helps us see things more clearly.

Jesus' teachings and actions were a light to all who listened because they helped people see what God is like. Jesus' followers today come to know who God is by listening to the teachings of Jesus, the Light of the World.

Jesus draws on people's experience of light and its importance in their lives to describe the Church's task in the world. The Church is to be such a caring, happy, hopeful community of people that all people will be moved to live more caring, happy, hopeful lives. Jesus calls each of us in the Church to be a light to others. Our lives should be examples to everyone we meet. The Church is to be a light to the world. Those who see us should be able to learn about God by what we do and what we say.

Activity

Write a poem about light that suggests how light makes you feel or why light is important to you. Use any kind of poetry you like. Be sure to give your poem a title.

_____

_____

_____

_____

_____

_____

We Believe

The community of the Church is a light to the world. Every member of the Church is called to live a good life. In this way all people can see the true way to God and happiness.

Jesus and Light ～～～～～

A large crowd of people sat on the side of the mountain where Jesus had been teaching his disciples. Jesus sat where everyone could see and hear him. He had just finished talking about his way to be happy.

After a few moments, Jesus began to speak again. All the people became silent and listened to him.

"You are the **light of the world**," Jesus said to his disciples. "A city set on a hill cannot be hidden."

The people in the crowd had all seen cities and towns built high up on hills. Anyone could find a city on a hill.

"People do not light a lamp and then put it under a bushel basket," Jesus went on. "They set it on a stand where it gives light to everyone in the house."

Again the people could understand what Jesus was saying. They all used candles and oil lamps to light their homes.

"In the same way," Jesus told his disciples, "your light must shine before people. Let your good deeds show for all to see. Then all will praise God, your heavenly Father."

Based on Matthew 5:14–16

Activity

Read the Scripture story again. Circle all the words about light. Talk about the meanings of these images.

Vocabulary

light of the world: the lives of Jesus and his followers shining before others and lighting the way to God and happiness

✖ ✖ ✖ ✖ ✖ ✖ ✖ ✖ ✖ ✖ ✖ ✖

A Light in My Life

Hi! I'm José and I'm eleven years old. I live in Brooklyn with my mom and my older brother, whose name is Manuel.

You would really like Manuel. He's a cool guy. He's one of the best players on the high school basketball team. Sometimes he shoots baskets with me after school.

Some of Manuel's friends have quit school, but not Manuel. He studies hard so that he'll be able to go to college next year. He even helps me with my school work when I'm having a hard time.

Manuel has a job at a neighborhood grocery store on weekends. He doesn't make much money, but he often buys Mom and me presents.

I know that I can't be exactly like Manuel, but I study hard and try not to get into trouble. I try to help Mom out whenever I can.

Mom says that Manuel is a good example for me and my friends. I agree, but mostly I just think he is a great brother!

When I pray, I always thank God for Mom and for Manuel and I ask the Lord to help me follow Manuel's good example.

Lights to the World

Jesus calls each of us to be a light to others by the way we live.

When someone stands up for those who are not treated fairly, he or she is a light to the world.

When someone teaches others what they do not know, he or she is a light to the world.

When someone tells the truth and not a lie, he or she is a light to the world.

When someone is honest and refuses to cheat, he or she is a light to the world.

When someone cares when others are sad, he or she is a light to the world.

When someone reaches out to help others who are hurting, he or she is a light to the world.

When someone helps a friend with homework, he or she is a light to the world.

Activity

Tell about two different people who are lights in your life by completing the following sentences. Be sure to mention specific things that you see these persons doing.

1. _____ is a light in my life

   because I can see the way he or she

   _____.

2. _____ is a light in my life

   because I can see the way he or she

   _____

   _____.

The Day of Pentecost

When the day of Pentecost came, the followers of Jesus were all together in one place. Suddenly from heaven there came a sound like the rush of a violent wind. It filled the whole house where they were sitting. Tongues, as of fire, appeared among them, and came to rest on each of them. All of them were filled with the Holy Spirit.

Based on Acts of the Apostles 2:1–4

The Power of the Holy Spirit

Since the day of Pentecost, through the power of the Holy Spirit, the followers of Jesus were able to go out and preach about Jesus. They lived in communities where they shared everything in common. They tried not to be selfish. They cared for one another and helped strangers. They lived as Jesus had told them. Together they were an example to others and a light to the world.

When other people saw how the followers of Jesus lived together in kindness and generosity, they became curious. They wanted to hear about Jesus and his teachings. The number of Christians grew.

The Holy Spirit gave the early followers of Jesus the courage to let their light shine before others. In the same way, the Holy Spirit can give us the strength and courage we need to be a light for others. Jesus has called each of us to be a light for the world by what we say and do.

Activity

In many ways, the Holy Spirit is already helping you to be a light to the world. The inventory below will help you see how well you are doing. It can also give you some ideas on how you can do better. Place an **X** in the column that best describes you.

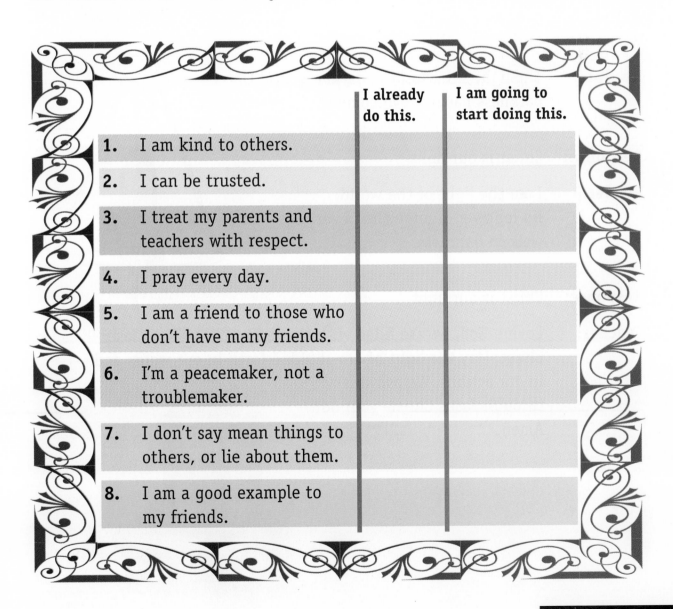

		I already do this.	I am going to start doing this.
1.	I am kind to others.		
2.	I can be trusted.		
3.	I treat my parents and teachers with respect.		
4.	I pray every day.		
5.	I am a friend to those who don't have many friends.		
6.	I'm a peacemaker, not a troublemaker.		
7.	I don't say mean things to others, or lie about them.		
8.	I am a good example to my friends.		

Praying About Light

Light has been a religious symbol for people since ancient times. The Jews of Jesus' time always kept a light burning in the Temple in Jerusalem, as a reminder to them that God was present there in a special way. In the same way, Catholics keep a light burning near the tabernacles in our churches as a reminder that Jesus is present there in a special way. And when we gather for prayer, we often light a candle as a sign of Christ's presence among us.

Pray the prayer below with your class.

Reader: The people who walked in darkness have seen a great light.

Isaiah 9:1

Response: Christ is our light.

Reader: The light shines in the darkness, and the darkness has not overcome it.

John 1:5

Response: Christ is our light.

Reader: I am the light of the world. No follower of mine shall ever walk in darkness.

Based on John 8:12

Response: Christ is our light.

Teacher: Loving God, we are filled with the light of your Son, Jesus Christ. May the light of Christ shine forth in our words and in our actions. We ask this through Jesus Christ, your Son. Amen.

Chapter Review

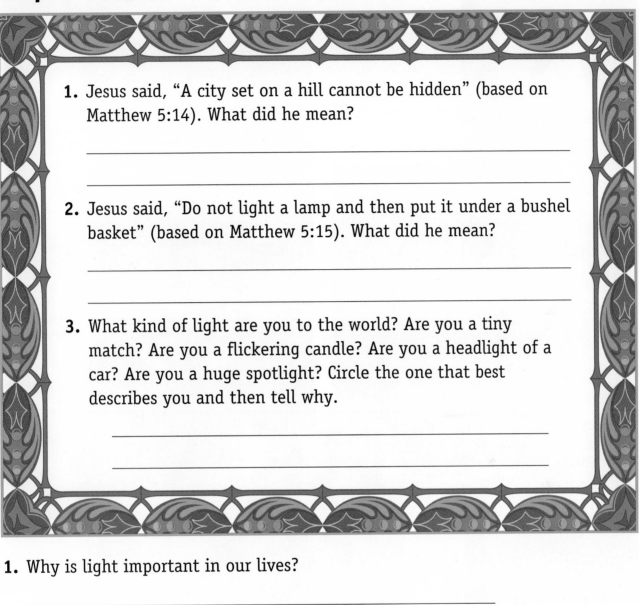

1. Jesus said, "A city set on a hill cannot be hidden" (based on Matthew 5:14). What did he mean?

   _____

   _____

2. Jesus said, "Do not light a lamp and then put it under a bushel basket" (based on Matthew 5:15). What did he mean?

   _____

   _____

3. What kind of light are you to the world? Are you a tiny match? Are you a flickering candle? Are you a headlight of a car? Are you a huge spotlight? Circle the one that best describes you and then tell why.

   _____

   _____

1. Why is light important in our lives?

   _____

   _____

2. Why were the disciples a light to the world?

   _____

   _____

   _____

   _____

Go out and be a light to all people so they can live in my love.

Based on Acts 13:47

3. Discuss how the community of the Church can become a brighter light for people today.

A Servant to the World

What are some things you like most about our world and some things you would like to change for the better?

Discuss

The pictures above show people doing special things. Think about what they are doing. How can their work help make the world a better place for people to live happily together?

Called to Be Builders

Jesus' example and words teach us to serve others. As Christians, we are each called to do what we can to help our neighbor. We are called to be of **service** to the whole world. We can do this by helping people who are in need. We can also serve by working with people who are trying to build a better world.

The service of some individuals can make a great difference in the world. We all benefit when someone works to stop war and fighting. Life is better for all people when someone works to stop starvation. But not all of us can be a part of such worldwide efforts.

Most of us work to make the world a better place within our own communities. When we serve one another, even in small ways, we make the world a better place in which to live.

Activity

Many Christians work to build a better world. Some are well-known people, such as Mother Teresa or Martin Luther King, Jr. Some are people who live in our own homes or communities.

On the lines below, write a description of someone you know who is working to build a better world by serving others.

_____

_____

_____

_____

_____

Vocabulary

service: work that helps others who need our care

✖ ✖ ✖ ✖ ✖ ✖ ✖ ✖ ✖ ✖ ✖

Jesus as Servant

Jesus and his disciples gathered for a meal on the night before he died. All the disciples sat around Jesus.

Then Jesus stood up. He picked up a towel and tied it around his waist. Jesus' friends were puzzled. "What is he doing?" they wondered.

Jesus poured water into a basin. He knelt on the floor and began to wash the feet of his disciples. He dried them with the towel at his waist.

"Why is Jesus washing our feet? That is the job of a servant," the disciples said to one another.

Peter did not want Jesus to kneel before him and wash his feet because he knew that Jesus was a very special person.

But Jesus said, "If I do not wash your feet, you will no longer be my disciple."

So Peter and all the other disciples let Jesus wash their feet. When Jesus finished, he put the water basin aside. He dried his hands and sat down at the table.

"Do you understand what I just did for you?" Jesus asked. No one answered. So Jesus explained.

"If I, your teacher and Lord, served you like this, then you must serve others as well. What I just did was to give you an example. You must do as I have done."

Based on John 13:1–17

Then and Now

In the time of Jesus, most people traveled from place to place by foot. When visitors arrived at someone's home, they were usually welcomed by having their feet washed. This task was carried out by one of the servants of the house.

In the Scripture story you just read, Jesus is not telling us to wash each others' feet. Rather, Jesus is telling us to serve one another in ways that are appropriate for our time. We are to serve one another even when we don't feel like it or when it's not convenient.

Discuss

How can fourth graders serve others as Jesus calls his followers to serve?

A Servant Church

Through Baptism we become members of the Catholic Church. When we follow the example and teachings of Jesus to serve others as he served, we are a servant Church. Service is an important part of the work of the Church.

The community of the Church is to be of service to the whole world. In remote areas, missionaries build schools. They try to help people grow more food so that they will not go hungry. The Church sends doctors and nurses to staff clinics and provide health care. In some countries, religious men and women operate shelters and schools for homeless children. These are some examples of a servant Church working to build a better world.

Our parish communities also work toward making our world a better place in which to live. Often parishes support worldwide Church efforts by sending clothing, money, or medical supplies to groups who work directly with the poor.

More often, parishes serve others within their own communities. Parish efforts might include feeding the homeless at a local shelter. A parish might also participate in resettling refugees or immigrants who have come to this country from other countries. In many parishes, parishioners visit the ill in hospitals or at home and help them with their yardwork or meals. In these and in many other ways, the parish Church is a servant Church.

Activity

On the lines below, name three things that your parish does to make the world a better place.

1. _____

2. _____

3. _____

Now name three things you would like your parish to begin doing to make the world a better place.

1. _____

2. _____

3. _____

We Believe

The Church is a servant Church. Jesus Christ calls the Church community to care for those in need and to work for those who want to build a better world.

Activity

Imagine a perfect world. Who would be in it? What would you get rid of? What would it feel like? Describe the better world you are imagining.

What Does Jesus Ask?

A better world will not just happen because we can imagine it. We need to work together to make it happen. By his teaching and example, Jesus helps us know how to build a better world. He asks us all to be servants to one another.

Jesus asks us to share in the work of the Church. We can participate in the acts of service that are part of our parish life. We can help organize and carry out works of service as part of our school life. We can work toward building a better world in our schools and in our homes.

Activity

Each of us can help create a better world *right now*. Think about the world you live in. As a fourth grader and a follower of Jesus, what are you willing to do to make your world a better place?

1. I will work to make my family a better family

   by _____

   _____ .

2. I will work to make my school a better school

   by _____

   _____ .

3. I will work to make my group of friends a better

   group by _____

   _____ .

4. I will work to make my parish a better parish by

   _____

   _____ .

5. I will work to make my neighborhood a better

   neighborhood by _____

   _____ .

Praying with Gestures

Throughout the history of the Church, people have used a variety of gestures in their prayer. It has always been important to Catholics to pray with their bodies as well as with words. Bowing and genuflecting, kneeling and standing, making the sign of the cross and folding our hands have long been prayerful gestures used by Catholics.

Pray the following prayer with your class, using the prayer gestures your teacher suggests.

Leader: We begin our prayer in the name of the Father, and of the Son, and of the Holy Spirit.

All: Amen.

Leader: Loving God, you are Creator of all. We offer you the work of our hands, for we are your servants.

All: We are your servants.

Leader: Generous God, you give us all that we need. Let us help others obtain all that they need. We offer you the work of our hands, for we are your servants.

All: We are your servants.

Leader: God of all people, we are your servant Church. Help us to work toward making the world a better place, for we are your servants.

All: We are your servants. We will build a better world. And we will do it in the name of the Father, and of the Son, and of the Holy Spirit. Amen.

Chapter Review

Look at the photographs. On the lines provided, tell how the people in each photograph are examples of the Servant Church.

_____   _____

_____   _____

_____   _____

_____

1. What is meant by *service*?

_____

2. How can we serve others as Jesus did?

_____

_____

_____

_____

_____

3. Discuss how Catholics can serve the world today.

> **Serve one another out of love.**
> **Based on Galatians 5:13**

UNIT 5 ORGANIZER

Celebrating and Serving

Chapter 17
The Sacrament of Reconciliation

Name the four parts to the sacrament of Reconciliation.

1. _____
2. _____
3. _____
4. _____

Chapter 18
Unity Through the Eucharist

Name any two of the eight signs of unity found in the celebration of the Eucharist.

1. _____
2. _____

Chapter 19
A Light to the World

Name two ways the early Christians were a light to the world.

1. _____
2. _____

Chapter 20
A Servant to the World

Name two ways Christians are called to serve others.

1. _____
2. _____

UNIT **5** REVIEW

Match the words in Column A with the definitions in Column B.

Column A

1. examination of conscience
2. absolution
3. Corinthians
4. Penance
5. service

Column B

_____ the people who lived in Corinth, a city in Greece

_____ thinking about what we have said and done and how we may have sinned

_____ work that helps others who need our care

_____ a prayer of forgiveness for sins prayed by the priest in the sacrament of Reconciliation

_____ another name for the sacrament of Reconciliation

Fill in the missing words to complete each sentence.

1. When we celebrate Reconciliation, we p ___ ___ ___ and make an examination of conscience, we c ___ ___ ___ ___ ___ ___ our sins to the p ___ ___ ___ ___ ___ , we accept a p ___ ___ ___ ___ ___ ___ , we express our s ___ ___ ___ ___ ___ , and we r ___ ___ ___ ___ ___ ___ absolution from the priest.

2. Saint Paul called the Church the B ___ ___ ___ of C ___ ___ ___ ___ ___ .

3. We gather at the E ___ ___ ___ ___ ___ ___ ___ to celebrate our u ___ ___ ___ ___ and to help it grow.

4. The community of the Church is a l ___ ___ ___ ___ to the

w ___ ___ ___ ___. Every member of the Church is called to live a

g ___ ___ ___ l ___ ___ ___.

5. All C ___ ___ ___ ___ ___ ___ ___ ___ ___ belong to the one

Body of Christ the C ___ ___ ___ ___ ___.

Write an X next to the correct examples of how the Church serves people
and tries to build a better world.

_____ sending missionaries to teach people about Jesus

_____ inventing larger airplanes

_____ opening health clinics in poor countries

_____ sending clothing to poor areas

_____ providing shelter for homeless children

_____ opening more grocery stores

_____ teaching people how to grow better crops

Use the words below to complete the following sentence.

followers	God	Jesus	Light of the World	happiness

_____, the _____, and the lives of his

_____ shine before others, lighting the way to _____

and _____.

LEARNING to SAY "I'M SORRY" RESPONDING with FORGIVENESS

Conflict or disagreements occur in all relationships. Feelings are often hurt by what is said or done. As followers of Jesus, we are called to be forgiving of those who have hurt us, and to ask forgiveness of those whom we have hurt. Saying "I'm sorry" and "It's okay, I forgive you" are important words of forgiveness and reconciliation. These words are not always easy to say, especially when the hurt feeling still exists. Jesus promises that he will be with us. Jesus will help heal the hurt we feel. Jesus will give us the strength to be forgiving even when it is difficult.

APOLOGIZING

What you say and how you say it are both very important parts of an apology. A helpful apology begins with "I'm sorry," followed by what it is you are sorry about. For example: "I'm sorry I hurt your feelings when I called you a name." The tone of voice is also important. A sincere voice tone suggests that the person really means what he or she is saying.

Apologies mean very little if the words of forgiveness are not followed by a change in what is said and done. If we continue to do the things that are hurtful, our apology is of little value in bringing healing to the relationship.

When someone apologizes, he or she is asking for our forgiveness. When we accept someone's apology, we are telling the other person that we do forgive him or her. The words we choose might sound like these:

"It's okay." I forgive you."

"I forgive you."

"Let's be friends again."

I'M SORRY I TALKED BACK TO YOU, MOM..

I FORGIVE YOU, LISA. I KNOW YOU DIDN'T MEAN WHAT YOU SAID.

I'M SORRY I PUSHED IN FRONT OF YOU IN LINE.

THAT'S OKAY I FORGIVE YOU.

Can You Help Lisa and Melanie?

Lisa and Melanie have been good friends for a long time. Lately they have not been getting along very well. Melanie has been playing with someone else at recess and Lisa feels left out. Whenever Lisa asks to play, Melanie tells her that only two people can play what she and her other friend are playing. Lisa's feelings are hurt. She tries to get back at Melanie by getting her other friends to dislike Melanie. Both Lisa and Melanie end up being angry at each other.

Let's suppose that Lisa is sorry and wants to apologize to Melanie. Use the speech balloons below to tell what Lisa could say and how Melanie might respond.

Apologizing is an important first step in reconciling. What else needs to happen between the girls for healing to occur?

_____

_____

_____

OPENING DOORS
A Take-Home Magazine™

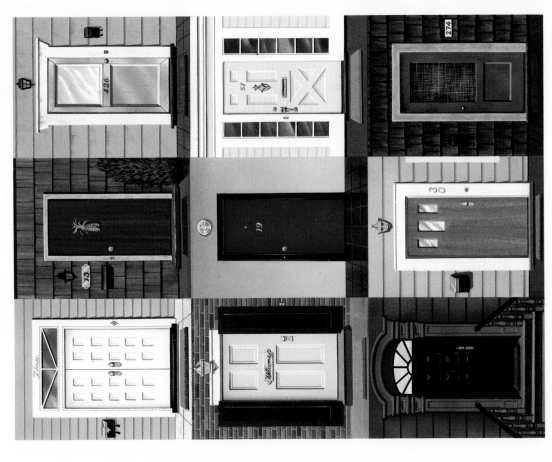

Growing Closer

AS A SIGN OF FAMILY UNITY and sense of Christian mission, plan an act of service for others. Everyone in the family should participate. The following are suggestions.

- Write notes or send greeting cards to someone who needs words of comfort or cheer.

- Do without a special treat. Donate the money to a shelter for the homeless or other charitable organization.

- Volunteer the family to help serve a meal at a shelter.

- Invite someone who is lonely as a guest for a family meal. Make this a special occasion by sharing your family's blessing cup.

Looking Ahead

Take advantage of the leisure days of summer to share with your child the hopes and dreams you have for each other. May you walk safely in the light and warmth of the summer sun.

Family Gathering

After the resurrection, Jesus appeared to his followers often at mealtime. The story of Emmaus (Luke 24:13-35), when Jesus walked with two disciples and broke bread with them reminds us of Jesus' presence when we celebrate the Eucharist.

It also reminds us that Jesus, the risen Lord, is with us always and everywhere.

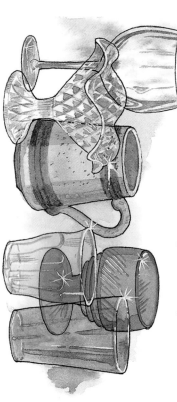

The gathering and sharing of the family meal symbolize and remind us of Christ's presence with us in our weekly routine. To help your family make at least one meal a month a sacramental occasion, you may want to adopt the sharing of the blessing cup described on page 3. Some families have adopted this ritual and have adapted prayers and types of sharing to fit their family needs.

Review with your child the names and uses of the vessels used during the Mass.

- The cruets are bottles which hold the wine and water brought to the altar during the Offertory procession.

- The chalice is the sacred cup in which wine is consecrated.

- The paten is the plate which holds the bread that is consecrated.

- The ciborium is a container used to hold hosts for communion distribution and for reservation in the tabernacle.

During prayer at mealtime, each person in the family drinks from a cup that your family has designated as the family blessing cup. The cup can be shared at every family meal or reserved for birthdays, anniversaries, holidays, or other occasions that your family considers special: when a visitor is dining with you, when someone brings home good news, when you want to welcome the first day of vacation.

Your family may also choose to share the blessing cup when family peace has been disturbed by quarrels, tension, bad news, or sickness. As you say a traditional or spontaneous prayer, each person drinks from the cup. Through this ritual your family will be reminded of bonds of love, unity, and peace.

Blessing cups are sold in religious goods stores or you may wish to use a family heirloom. Any glass, cup, or drinking vessel can be used. The cup should be set aside in a special place. Any beverage may be used, but fruit juice, water, or milk may be the most symbolic because of their nourishing and nurturing qualities.

Sacred Vessels

The next time you are in church draw your child's attention to the tabernacle. Explain that in this safe-like box is the Blessed Sacrament.

Tell your child we genuflect when we enter the pews in church as a sign of respect and reverence of Christ's presence with us.

Go in Peace

The sacrament of the Eucharist calls us to unity and peace. The sacramental ritual symbolizes and renews the unity for which Jesus prayed at the Last Supper. The Eucharist is also the sacrament of Christ's total self-giving. We share in the Eucharist and are called to service of others.

The Mass concludes with the Blessing and the Dismissal. We are blessed and sent out to be a blessing to others. It may be a simple or solemn blessing or a prayer over the people.

The following words are one of the solemn blessings during Ordinary Time. It is from the Blessing of Aaron in the Old Testament, the Hebrew Scriptures.

> May the Lord bless you and keep you. R/Amen.
>
> May his face shine upon you, and be gracious to you. R/Amen.
>
> May he look upon you with kindness, and give you his peace. R/Amen.
>
> May almighty God bless you, the Father, and the Son, and the Holy Spirit. R/Amen.

To Love and Serve

When Latin was used in the Mass, the priest dismissed the people with the words *Ite missa est.* The word Mass is derived from the word *missa.* It is interesting that the English word "mission" comes from the same root.

At the Dismissal of Mass we are given the mission to love and serve the Lord faithfully as we do the work of Christ in the world.

Celebrating the Journey

Leader: We have learned that the gift of grace fills our lives with God's presence. We witness God's abundant love for us in one another and in creation. Let us pause and remember some of the good things God has done for us. (Pause.)

Reader: Remembering God's goodness, let us listen closely to a reading from Paul's First Letter to the Corinthians.

I give thanks to God always for you because of the grace of God that has been given to you in Jesus. For in every way you have been blest in him, in your speech and in your knowledge. The witness to Christ has been strengthened in you so that you are not in want of any spiritual gift as you wait for the return of the Lord Jesus. He will also strengthen you right up to the end, so that you may be blameless on the day of our Lord Jesus Christ. God is faithful and it was by God that you were called into friendship with Jesus our Lord.

Based on 1Corinthians 1:4–9

The word of the Lord.

All: Thanks be to God.

Leader: Lord Jesus, we thank you for being present to us on our journey of faith. Stay with us always, guiding us and forgiving us, so that we may share with others the many gifts we have received from God our Father.

All: Amen.

Our Church Celebrates Advent

The Journey to Bethlehem

During Advent, we get ready for Jesus to come into our lives at Christmas. Part of the Advent story is the journey of Mary and Joseph to Bethlehem.

At that time the ruler of their land ordered all people to return to their hometowns to be counted in a census of the whole country. Bethlehem was Joseph's hometown, so Mary and Joseph had to travel there.

Mary would soon give birth to her baby. Joseph was worried about Mary, because he loved her very much, and knew the trip to Bethlehem would be hard for her. Joseph felt sad about the trip, but he believed that God would watch over them and help take care of Mary.

Mary was worried about Joseph, too, because she loved him very much. She knew the trip would be tiring for him. Mary also felt sad that she and Joseph would have to travel to Bethlehem.

But she, too, believed that God would watch over them. Mary knew that God would help her take care of Joseph.

Based on Luke 2:1–5

Journeying Toward Jesus

When Mary and Joseph traveled to Bethlehem, they probably took only what they really needed. Bringing a lot of things would have made the trip more difficult.

During the season of Advent, we make a spiritual journey toward Jesus, who will be with us in a new way on Christmas. Like Joseph and Mary, we, too, must decide what will help us on our way. We can ask, "What must I take with me if I want to journey toward Jesus? What must I leave behind?"

Activity

Travel along the road above. It leads to Jesus. Read each word along your way. Decide if you will take it with you as you travel or leave it behind. Then fill in the blanks below with the words.

Take it along

1. _____
2. _____
3. _____
4. _____

Leave it behind

1. _____
2. _____
3. _____
4. _____

The Advent Season

Colors are important to us. Some colors make us feel joyful and happy. Other colors seem quiet and peaceful.

The Church uses a different color during each of its special seasons. The colors tell us something about the meaning of each season.

The season of Advent is a prayerful time. It is a time of waiting and hopefulness. We look forward eagerly to the new coming of Jesus at Christmastime. We also prepare our hearts for the coming of Jesus when he returns in glory.

During Advent, the priest wears purple vestments. The Advent wreath in church has three purple candles and one pink candle. Purple is a sign of preparation and change. Pink is a sign of hope and joy. These colors help us remember that Advent is a time to prepare for Jesus by showing our love for others and having hope in God's promises. As we prepare for God's gift of Jesus at Christmas, we give the gift of ourselves to others during Advent.

Activity

Design an Advent banner. Imagine that your banner will hang in church. What color or colors will you use? What symbols or words will you choose to help the people of your parish celebrate this Advent season?

Visitors for Christmas

Tina and Carlos heard their mother talking excitedly on the phone in Spanish. Although the children knew many words in Spanish, their mother was talking too quickly for them to understand what she was saying. They knew that something important was going on.

Finally, Mrs. Ramírez hung up the phone and clapped her hands, "*Los abuelitos vienen para las Navidades!*" Then she repeated the good news in English, "Your grandparents are coming for Christmas!"

Tina and Carlos were surprised. They had not seen their grandparents in three years. Carlos was too young to remember visiting them at Christmas in Mexico City when Tina was in first grade. But Tina remembered every minute of the exciting trip. She remembered helping her Mexican cousins set up the *nacimiento*, the Christmas scene of the manger where Jesus was born.

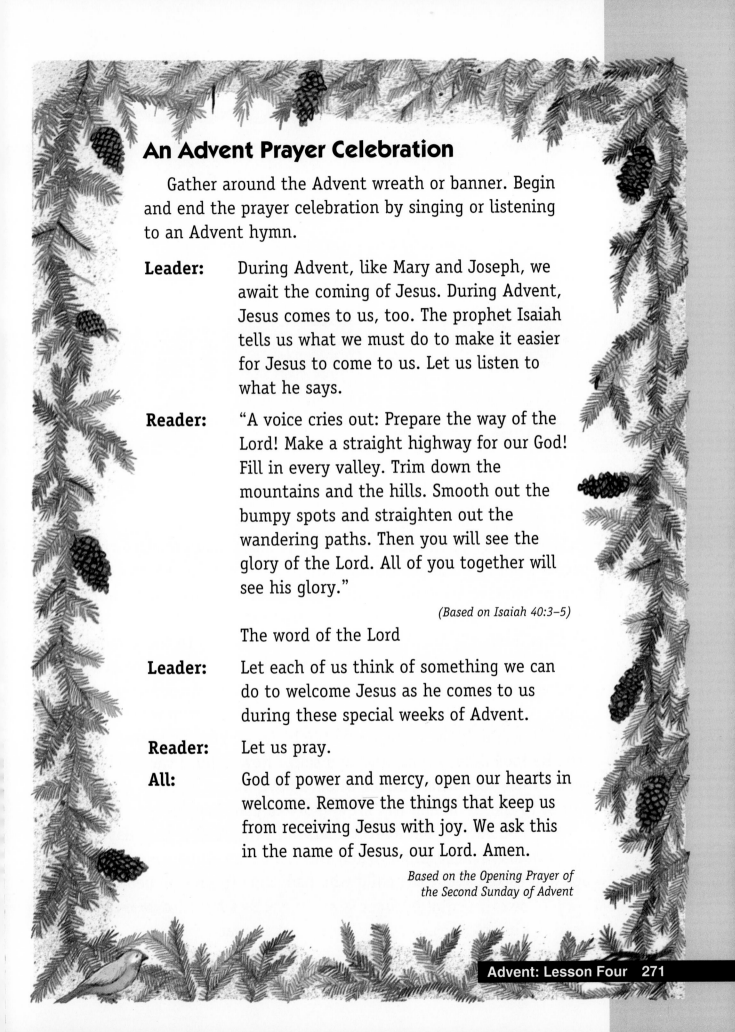

An Advent Prayer Celebration

Gather around the Advent wreath or banner. Begin and end the prayer celebration by singing or listening to an Advent hymn.

Leader: During Advent, like Mary and Joseph, we await the coming of Jesus. During Advent, Jesus comes to us, too. The prophet Isaiah tells us what we must do to make it easier for Jesus to come to us. Let us listen to what he says.

Reader: "A voice cries out: Prepare the way of the Lord! Make a straight highway for our God! Fill in every valley. Trim down the mountains and the hills. Smooth out the bumpy spots and straighten out the wandering paths. Then you will see the glory of the Lord. All of you together will see his glory."

(Based on Isaiah 40:3–5)

The word of the Lord

Leader: Let each of us think of something we can do to welcome Jesus as he comes to us during these special weeks of Advent.

Reader: Let us pray.

All: God of power and mercy, open our hearts in welcome. Remove the things that keep us from receiving Jesus with joy. We ask this in the name of Jesus, our Lord. Amen.

Based on the Opening Prayer of the Second Sunday of Advent

Our Church Celebrates Christmas

Our Savior Is Born

Many, many years ago, God made a promise. God promised that all people would be brought closer to God. God's own Son became a human being to bring God to all people. And so Jesus, the Son of God, was born. We celebrate his birth on Christmas.

After Jesus was born, Mary and Joseph took him to the Temple in Jerusalem to present him to God. At that time an old man named Simeon was in the Temple, too. God had promised Simeon that he would not die until he had seen the special person who would come to save the world. When Simeon saw the baby, he knew who the child was. He took Jesus in his arms and said, "Now, Lord, I can die in peace. I have seen the one for whom I have waited so long. He will be a light to the world and will bring glory to your people."

Mary and Joseph met another person in the Temple that day. They met a woman named Anna. When she saw Jesus, Anna gave thanks to God and talked about the child who had come to save all people.

Based on Luke 2:25–38

The Light of the World

On Christmas we remember what Simeon and Anna said about Jesus. We remember that he is the savior who brings people to God as God had promised.

We often call Jesus the Light of the World. The candles and lights on Christmas remind us that Jesus can bring new light to our world.

At Christmas Mass we hear these words reminding us of Jesus: "The people who walked in darkness have seen a great light. The light brings brightness to those who live in sadness. For a child is born who will save us and lead us."

(Based on Isaiah 9:1, 5–6)

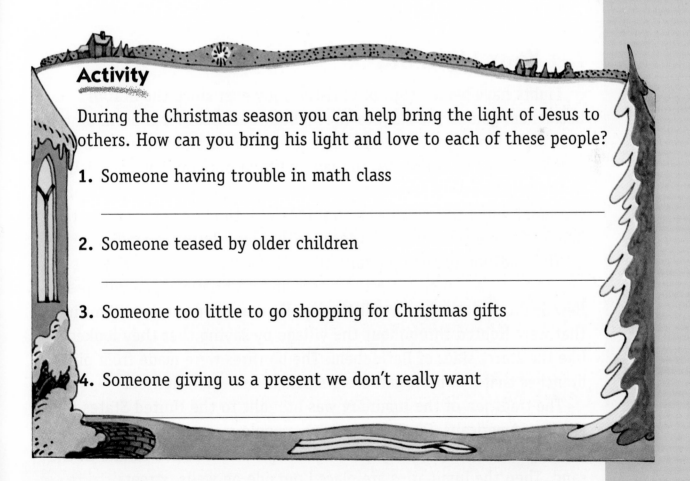

Activity

During the Christmas season you can help bring the light of Jesus to others. How can you bring his light and love to each of these people?

1. Someone having trouble in math class

_____

2. Someone teased by older children

_____

3. Someone too little to go shopping for Christmas gifts

_____

4. Someone giving us a present we don't really want

_____

Let Your Light Shine

Lights have been a sign of Christmas joy ever since the Star of Bethlehem guided the Magi to the stable where Jesus was born. Since that night long ago, Christians have used candles and fire as a way to welcome Jesus at Christmas. In many parts of our country, especially in the Southwestern states, luminaries are used to remind people of the night when the world was brightened by the light of Jesus' birth. Luminaries are small paper lanterns with a long-burning candle.

The tradition of the luminary in North America is over 400 years old. In 1534, a Franciscan priest wrote about Christmas in a village in New Spain, which we now call Mexico. He described the small bonfires that were lighted throughout the village by saying that they looked like the starry skies of Bethlehem. The bonfires were made from pine branches that had been gathered, stocked, and then lighted.

The tradition of the luminary was brought to the United States by Mexican Americans. On Christmas Eve, people make luminaries by pouring sand into a small paper bag and placing a votive candle in the sand. Then the luminaries are placed outside on walls, streets, sidewalks, and church steps.

At night, the candles are lighted and the glow from the luminaries seems to light up the whole town. In some places, luminaries light the way for families walking to midnight Mass. The legend of the luminary says that the light is a sign to the Christ Child, the *Santo Niño*. The light says that he and his family are welcome and will find a home in the village.

Jesus once told his friends about light. Jesus said, "You are a light to the world. Make your light shine, so that others will see the good that you do and will praise your Father in heaven" (Based on Matthew 5:14, 16).

Jesus called his followers to be examples for others of his love and care. At Christmas, we let our light shine in a special way to welcome Jesus.

Activity

On each of the luminaries, write one way that you can be an example to others of Jesus' love and care.

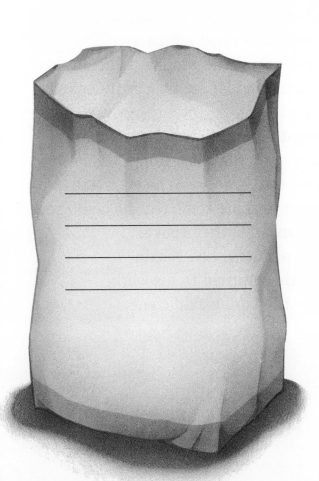
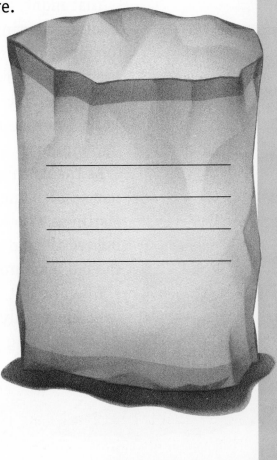

Martin the Cobbler

Adapted from a story by Leo Tolstoy

There once was a cobbler named Martin. Martin knew every pair of boots in the village. He could recognize who was walking outside by the sound of their boots.

One day, a holy traveler stopped at Martin's shop. "Please make a new binding for this old, old Bible," he said. "I am greatly honored," Martin began, "but you must take this book to someone else. You see, God and I have not been getting on well."

And what he said was true. Martin had had much sadness in his life. Both his wife and his sons had died. In his great sorrow, Martin grew bitter. He blamed God for all the hard things in his life.

"Perhaps you are sad and without hope now, because you live only for yourself," the holy man explained. "Live for God, Martin. He gives you life."

That night, as Martin was reading his Bible, he heard a voice: "Martin, Martin, look out into the street tomorrow for I shall come." Martin was not sure whether the voice was real or just a dream.

The next day he sat nearer the window as he did his work. When he heard unfamiliar boots, Martin looked up, hoping to see the Lord.

As the morning went on, Martin saw an old man named Stepanich sweeping the snow from the sidewalk. Martin saw how tired, cold, and weak he was. Martin invited the old man in to share some tea. He could see the old man grow stronger as they spoke.

When he left, Stepanich thanked Martin wholeheartedly. Martin returned to his work, wondering when the Lord would come.

When he glanced up later, Martin was surprised to see a young woman, poorly dressed, trying to keep herself and a small baby warm. Martin called to her to come in. Martin offered her some warm porridge. Then he gave her one of his heavy cloaks to wear. The woman was so touched by Martin's kindness that there were tears in her eyes as she thanked him.

Toward evening, Martin viewed another scene through his window. A young boy had taken an apple from the basket of an old woman. The woman was shaking the boy and scolding him loudly. Martin left his shop. "We must forgive as the Lord forgives us," Martin instructed the old woman. As Martin spoke, the old woman and the young boy both changed. Martin watched as they went off together, chatting happily as they walked.

That evening, Martin settled himself to read the Bible again. He was disappointed that the Lord had not come as God had promised. Again he heard the voice, "Martin, Martin, don't you know me?"

"Who are you?" asked Martin.

Discuss

1. Whose voice do you think Martin heard?

2. Listen to the end of the story. Did the Lord come to Martin? How?

A Classroom Play

The story of Martin the Cobbler can be divided into six acts.

Act One: Martin Meets a Holy Traveler
Act Two: Martin Receives a Message
Act Three: Martin Helps an Old Man
Act Four: Martin Cares For a Woman and Her Baby
Act Five: Martin Teaches Forgiveness
Act Six: Martin Recognizes the Lord

These steps will help you act out the story.

1. Your teacher will divide the class into groups. Choose the act or acts your group will work on.

2. Write the names of the characters in your act and what they will say. Choose members of your group to play these parts.

3. Find props and costumes for the play.

4. Practice the play, act by act. Be sure to include all the important parts of the story.

5. Invite other classes to see the play.

A Christmas Prayer Celebration

Your teacher will divide the class into four groups. Each group will be given a passage to read from the Bible. Read the passage aloud and talk about what it means to you. Then choose one member of your group to read the passage during the prayer celebration.

Teacher: Long ago, God promised to bring light to the world. That light is Jesus. The darkness of our world today needs the light of God. Let us listen to God's messages about light and love.

Reader 1: Read John 1:3–5 as the teacher lights the first candle.

Reader 2: Read Luke 2:29–32 as the teacher lights the second candle.

Reader 3: Read Matthew 4:16 as the teacher lights the third candle.

Reader 4: Read Matthew 25:37–40 as the teacher lights the fourth candle.

All: Loving God, during this Christmas season we are filled with the new light of your love. By the coming among us of your Son, Jesus, may the light of faith shine in our words and actions. We ask this through Christ, our Lord. Amen.

Based on the Opening Prayer of the Christmas Mass

Our Church Celebrates Lent

Ash Wednesday

Jesus went to the desert for forty days to pray and fast. While he was in the desert, Jesus overcame the temptations of the devil. Jesus left the desert and returned to Galilee, where he had grown up, to begin his ministry of preaching the good news about God. This is what Jesus told the people: "The time has come. The Kingdom of God is near. Turn away from your sins and believe the good news!"

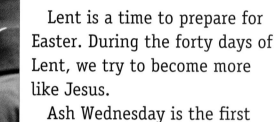

Based on Mark 1:12–15

Lent is a time to prepare for Easter. During the forty days of Lent, we try to become more like Jesus.

Ash Wednesday is the first day of Lent. On Ash Wednesday, we go to Mass. During the Liturgy of the Word, we learn that Lent is a time when Jesus calls us to say that we are sorry for our sins and want to change the way we have been living.

After the homily, the priest or other minister makes the sign of the cross on our foreheads with blessed ashes. The ashes are a sign that we are ready to change our lives. As we are signed with the ashes, the priest or minister says, "Turn away from sin and be faithful to the gospel." The gospel is the good news about Jesus' life and teachings. Jesus wants us to trust and depend on what he has taught us about God's love and forgiveness.

During Lent, we remember that Jesus died on the cross. Jesus sacrificed his life so that we can live forever with God. On Ash Wednesday, we can decide to make sacrifices during lent to show our love for Jesus. Our sacrifices during Lent help us prepare to celebrate Jesus' resurrection on Easter.

There are three kinds of sacrifices we can make during Lent. We can pray, fast, and do good works. We can find a special time each day to pray. We can fast by giving up a favorite treat or television show. We can look for ways to help others during Lent.

On Ash Wednesday, we remember these words from Scripture, "Do good and share what you have. God is pleased by these sacrifices" (Based on Hebrews 13:16).

Activity

Our Lenten sacrifices help God's kingdom of peace, love, and justice grow in the world. Complete the chart by writing your plan for Lent.

Lenten Sacrifices	My Lenten Plan
Prayer	_____ _____
Fasting	_____ _____
Good Works	_____ _____

Jesus Teaches Us to Follow Him

When the disciples decided to travel with Jesus, he taught them many things along the way. They began to understand what it means to be a follower of Jesus. Jesus taught his followers how important it is to trust his Father for all that they need.

Jesus once said to them, "Look at the flowers of the field and the birds in the air. They don't worry or work. Yet my Father cares for them. Your heavenly Father knows all that you need, even before you ask. He will care for you" (based on Matthew 6:26–30).

Jesus taught his followers that traveling with him means giving up always having to be first and having their own way. Jesus taught his friends an important lesson when he said, "If anyone among you wants to be great, he or she must be your servant. Anyone who wants to be first must take care of everyone else. I came not to be served but to serve others" (based on Matthew 20:26–28).

Jesus often spoke about loving God and loving others. He told his followers that they must even love those who were unkind to them. Jesus' words to them were, "Love your enemies. Do good to those who hate you. Be kind to those who hurt you and pray for those who treat you badly" (based on Luke 6:27–28).

Think about what these words of Jesus teach you about being his follower. What are some changes you can make in your life during this Lenten season that will help you to be a better follower of Jesus?

Activity

1. As we journey with Jesus, we need to make good choices in our life. Look at the road signs below. Read the list of good choices we can make as we journey with Jesus. Draw lines to match the signs with the suggestions.

When you decide to do something good, don't give up.

Let other people have their way sometimes.

Stay away from places and people who are not good for you.

2. Under each sign below, write some good choices that will help you follow Jesus.

_____

_____

_____

_____

_____

_____

_____

_____

_____

Traveling with Jesus

Each year Jesus traveled to Jerusalem to celebrate a special feast with his family and friends. This feast was called Passover. On Jesus' last trip to Jerusalem before his death and resurrection, the disciples were worried about him. They knew that some people wanted to hurt him. The disciples loved Jesus very much. They told Jesus that it was not safe for him to go to Jerusalem. But Jesus knew that he must go.

During the journey other people asked Jesus if they could go with him. Jesus told the people that it would not be easy to follow him. He said, "When you decide to follow me, you must not keep looking back when things get hard. You must not make excuses and say that you have other important things to do. Come now and tell everyone about the reign of God" (based on Luke 9:57–62).

Our Journey with Jesus

During Lent we journey with Jesus. Jesus said that it would not be easy to follow him. We think about Jesus' words. We look at how we are living and ask Jesus to help us. We try to help others, even when it means we must change our plans. We try not to make excuses or to find other things to do when it is time to pray. We ask Jesus to give us the courage to do what is right even when it is hard.

Activity

Look at the picture below. It shows what someone is doing to follow Jesus. Then on the lines below, write a prayer about how you can be a good follower of Jesus. Give your prayer a title.

_____

_____

_____

_____

_____

_____

_____

_____

_____

_____

_____

_____

_____

The Way of the Cross

During Lent, Catholics pray a special prayer that helps us remember Jesus' journey to Calvary, where he died. This prayer is called the Way of the Cross. People began to pray the Way of the Cross many years ago by walking along the route Jesus traveled and stopping to pray and remember the things that happened to Jesus. In our parish we can pray the Way of the Cross by walking from station to station in church.

Leader: We adore You, O Christ, and we bless You.
All: Because by Your holy cross You have redeemed the world.

The First Station ~ Jesus Is Condemned to Die

Reader: Dear Jesus, help me love God always and to trust in God's plan for me and my life.

The Second Station ~ Jesus Accepts the Cross

Reader: Dear Jesus, when I am asked to do difficult things, help me follow your example.

The Third Station ~ Jesus Falls the First Time

Reader: Dear Jesus, help me finish the things I begin, even when I do not want to.

The Fourth Station ~ Jesus Meets His Mother

Reader: Dear Jesus, remind me to be thankful for the love and support of my parents.

The Fifth Station ~ Simon Helps Jesus Carry the Cross

Reader: Dear Jesus, help me always to be willing to help those who are in need.

The Sixth Station ~ Veronica Wipes the Face of Jesus

Reader: Dear Jesus, teach me to show love and kindness to others without being asked.

The Seventh Station ~ Jesus Falls the Second Time

Reader: Dear Jesus, keep me from giving in to the temptations of life. Help my love for you grow.

The Eighth Station ~ Jesus Meets the Women of Jerusalem

Reader: Dear Jesus, keep me from bringing pain or sadness to the people who love me.

The Ninth Station ~ Jesus Falls the Third Time

Reader: Dear Jesus, give me the courage and strength to follow you always.

The Tenth Station ~ Jesus Is Stripped of His Garments

Reader: Dear Jesus, help me stand up for people who are being treated unfairly.

The Eleventh Station ~ Jesus Is Nailed to the Cross

Reader: Dear Jesus, teach me to forgive those who have hurt me.

The Twelfth Station ~ Jesus Dies on the Cross

Reader: Dear Jesus, thank you for sacrificing your life on the cross for all of us, your brothers and sisters. Help me love you always.

The Thirteenth Station ~ Jesus Is Taken Down from the Cross

Reader: Dear Jesus, help me comfort anyone who is sad or lonely.

The Fourteenth Station ~ Jesus Is Buried in the Tomb

Reader: Dear Jesus, you promised you would rise from the dead. Teach me to have hope in all your promises.

The Fifteenth Station ~ Jesus Rises from the Dead

Reader: Dear Jesus, we rejoice in your resurrection to new life. Alleluia! May our lives be a sign to others of your love and peace.

A Lenten Mobile

Make a Lenten mobile to help you remember how to be a better follower of Jesus. To make your mobile you will need these materials.

- a plastic hanger or three plastic straws crossed and joined together
- construction paper, crayons, and scissors to make symbols
- string to attach the symbols to the mobile

Choose a personal Lenten practice for each week of Lent. Make a paper symbol for each practice. Hang a new symbol on your mobile each week to remind you to do the Lenten practice you have chosen.

Here are some ideas for practices and symbols. You can use these or make up your own.

Week 1: Show signs of love to family members.

Week 2: Stop doing something that is a bad habit.

Week 3: Reach out to others in service and friendship.

Week 4: Take special care of God's gifts of creation.

Week 5: Remember how much Jesus loves you.

Week 6: Take extra time to pray during Holy Week.

A Lenten Prayer Celebration

Teacher: Lent is a time to grow and change. It is a time to ask ourselves how we can follow Jesus more closely. During Lent, the Church encourages us to find ways to pray, to make sacrifices, and to do good works. Let us listen to what Jesus tells us in the Gospel of Matthew.

Reader 1: Jesus says, "When you pray, don't act like showoffs who just want people to notice them. Instead, when you pray, go to your room or a quiet place and pray to your Father in private" (based on Matthew 6:5–6).

All: Jesus, help us find time to pray this Lent.

Reader 2: Jesus says, "When you make sacrifices, don't look sad and gloomy. Showoffs do that so everyone will know they are making a sacrifice. Instead, be pleasant and cheerful so that no one but you and God will know" (based on Matthew 6:16–18).

All: Jesus, help us to have the courage this Lent to give up some of the things we want so that others can have what they need.

Reader 3: Jesus says, "When you do kind deeds, be careful you are not doing them so that other people will praise you. No, when you do works of mercy, don't even let your left hand know what your right hand is doing. This will please your heavenly Father and God will reward you for all you do" (based on Matthew 6:1–4).

All: Jesus, help us find ways this Lent to care for and serve others.

Our Church Celebrates Holy Week

Passion Sunday

Jesus and his disciples journeyed to Jerusalem. When they got near the city, Jesus sent two of his disciples ahead of him. He said, "Go into the next village, where you will find a donkey that has never been ridden. Untie the donkey and bring it to me. If anyone asks what you are doing, tell them that the Lord needs the donkey."

The disciples went off and found a donkey tied to a gate. While they were untying it, some people asked, "What are you doing?" They answered just as Jesus had told them to do.

They led the donkey to Jesus. They put their cloaks on its back and helped Jesus get on. As Jesus rode along, the people spread their coats on the road in front of him. Others cut leafy branches from the trees. They laid them in front of Jesus and waved them in the air shouting, "Hosanna! Blessed is the one who comes in the name of the Lord! Hosanna to God in heaven!"

Based on Mark 11:1–10

Passion Sunday is the first day of Holy Week. On Passion Sunday, we remember that Jesus was greeted like a king when he came to Jerusalem. The people ran to meet Jesus and called out words of praise to him. They cried, "Hosanna!" which means "Praise be to the God who saves us."

On Passion Sunday, palms are blessed and given to everyone at Mass. We wave our palms as we walk in procession. We thank and praise God for Jesus. We remember that in the days after Jesus was welcomed like a king, he was arrested and put to death on the cross.

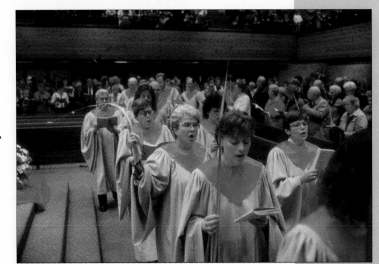

On Passion Sunday, the priest wears red vestments. The color red reminds us that Jesus suffered and died to save us from sin and death. During Holy Week, we remember Jesus' sacrifice.

Activity

Complete the sentences below by filling in the missing words.

1. _____ Sunday is the first day of

   _____ Week.

2. When Jesus came to _____, he was

   greeted like a _____ .

3. On Passion _____ , we receive blessed

   _____ .

4. During Holy Week, we remember that _____

   suffered and _____ to save us from

   _____ and death.

The Triduum

During Holy Week we celebrate the three holiest days of the Church year. These holy days are called the Triduum. The word *triduum* means "three days." In the Triduum, we walk with Jesus on his journey through death to new life. During the Triduum, we celebrate Holy Thursday, Good Friday, and Easter.

Holy Thursday

On Holy Thursday, we remember Jesus' Last Supper. Before the meal, Jesus washed his disciples' feet. Jesus did

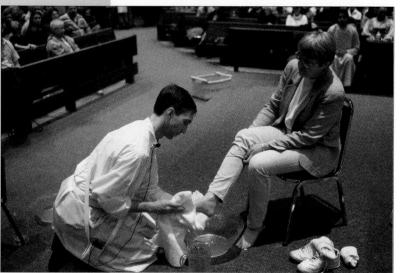

this to give his friends an example of how they must serve others. Jesus said, "What I have done, you must also do" (Based on John 13:15).

During Mass on Holy Thursday, we remember that Jesus gave us himself in the Eucharist for the first time at the Last Supper. In memory of him, we share Jesus' Body and Blood in the Eucharist.

Good Friday

On Good Friday, we gather for a special prayer service. There are no Masses on Good Friday. The prayer service begins at about three o'clock in the afternoon, as a reminder of the time when Jesus died. We listen to the story of Jesus' suffering and death. We are invited to show love and respect for the cross by kissing it, genuflecting before it, or touching it prayerfully with our hands. The Good Friday service ends with communion. We receive hosts that were blessed on Holy Thursday and kept in the tabernacle overnight. We leave the church in silence, to wait and watch for Jesus' resurrection.

Holy Saturday

On Holy Saturday, we prepare to welcome the risen Jesus. There are no Masses until night, when we celebrate the Easter Vigil. During the Easter Vigil, we light the Easter candle, which is a sign that Jesus is risen and gives light to the whole world. We listen to stories about God's love for his people since the time of Creation. We baptize and confirm new members of the Catholic community and renew our own Baptism promises. Finally, we welcome our new members to the Lord's table for the first time and we receive Eucharist with them.

Activity

Write **True** if the sentence is true. Write **False** if the sentence is false.

1. _____ The word *triduum* means "holy days."

2. _____ Jesus washed his disciples' feet to give them an example of service.

3. _____ Jesus gave us the Eucharist for the first time on Good Friday.

4. _____ We show respect for the cross on Good Friday.

5. _____ New members are baptized on Holy Thursday.

6. _____ We share the Eucharist in memory of Jesus.

7. _____ We baptize and confirm new members of the Catholic community at the Easter Vigil.

Our Church Celebrates Easter

An Easter Play

Reader 1: On the first day of the week, when it was still dark, Mary of Magdala went to the place where Jesus was buried. She saw that the stone had been rolled back from the entrance of the tomb. Mary ran to tell Peter and the other disciples.

Mary: They have taken Jesus from the tomb and I don't know where they have put him.

Reader 2: Peter and another disciple ran to the tomb. The other disciple looked in. He saw the cloths that had covered Jesus' body lying there. When Peter arrived, he went into the tomb and saw that the cloth that had covered Jesus' head was in a different place from the other cloths.

Reader 3: Then the other disciple followed his friend into the tomb. They saw the burial cloths and were amazed at what had happened. Then both disciples returned home.

Reader 4: But Mary stayed outside the tomb crying. She looked into the tomb and saw two angels sitting in the place where Jesus' body had been. One of the angels spoke to her.

Angel: Woman, why are you crying?

Mary: Someone has taken my Lord and I do not know where they have put him.

Reader 5: Mary turned around and saw Jesus, but she did not recognize him. She thought he was the gardener. Mary talked to the man.

Mary: Sir, if you carried Jesus away, tell me where you have laid him and I will go and get him.

Reader 6: Just then Jesus called out Mary's name. At once, she recognized him. Mary was filled with joy! She reached out to touch Jesus and called him by name.

Mary: Teacher!

Jesus: Go to my disciples, Mary, and tell them that I have risen and that I will soon return to my Father and your Father who is in heaven.

Reader 7: Mary went to the disciples as Jesus asked.

Mary: I have seen the Lord!

Based on John 20:1–18

Activity

To discover what we celebrate on Easter, write the letter in the alphabet that comes AFTER each letter in the puzzle.

I __ d __ r __ t __ r __   h __ r __

q __ h __ r __ d __ m __   e __ q __ n __ l __

s __ g __ d __   c __ d __ z __ c __   z __ m __ c __

r __ g __ z __ q __ d __ r __   g __ h __ r __

m __ d __ v __   k __ h __ e __ d __

v __ h __ s __ g __   t __ r __ .

The Story of Thomas

After Jesus died on the cross, his friends were confused. They had trouble believing that Jesus had risen from the dead and lives in a new way. Jesus visited them to help them believe. Here is a story of a time when the risen Jesus came to be with his followers.

On the night when Jesus rose from the dead, his disciples were together in a locked room. They were afraid because of what had happened to Jesus. Jesus came and stood before them. "Peace be with you," he said. Then Jesus showed his disciples his hands where he had been nailed to the cross. He showed them his side where he had been speared.

"It really is you, Jesus," they cried. They started talking with him all at once.

Thomas was not in the room with the other disciples. Later, when the disciples saw Thomas, they said, "Jesus is really alive! He was with us and we talked with him. He showed us his hands and his side. It really was Jesus!"

But Thomas shook his head. "I'll never believe that," he said, "unless I touch the wounds in his hands and his side."

A week later the disciples were together in the room again. This time Thomas was there, too. Again Jesus came and stood before them. "Peace be with you," he said.

Then he said to Thomas, "Come, touch my hands and my side. Believe what the others told you. I am alive."

Thomas prayed, "My Lord and my God."

Then Jesus said, "Thomas, you became a believer because you saw me. Blessed are those who have not seen me, but still believe."

Based on John 20:19–29

Activity

Use the secret code to find the words. The words make up a prayer to say when you find it hard to believe.

Secret Code

1	2	3	4	5	6	7	8	9	10	11	12	13
a	b	c	d	e	f	g	h	i	j	k	l	m

14	15	16	17	18	19	20	21	22	23	24	25	26
n	o	p	q	r	s	t	u	v	w	x	y	z

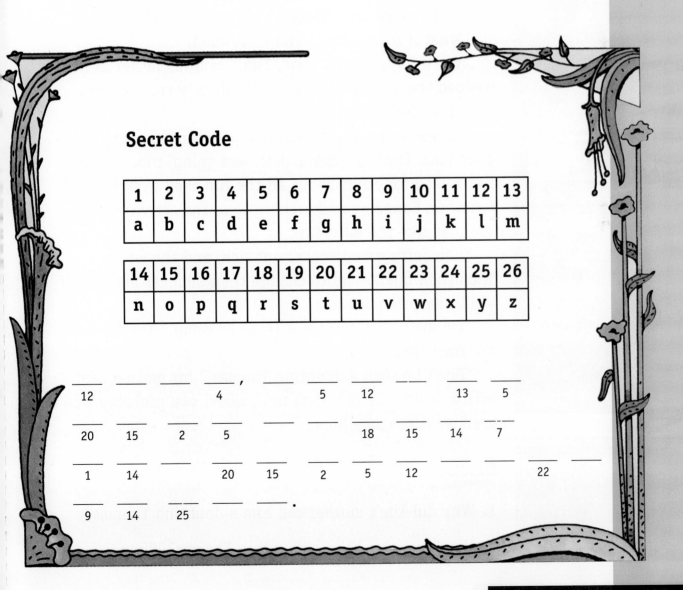

____ ____ ____ ____ ____ , ____ ____ ____ ____ ____ ____ ____ ____
12   4   5   12   13   5

____ ____ ____ ____   ____ ____ ____ ____
20   15   2   5   18   15   14   7

____ ____   ____ ____ ____ ____ ____   ____
1   14   20   15   2   5   12   22

____ ____ ____ .
9   14   25

A Chance to Trust

"But I won't know anybody," Tim said as he plopped his backpack into the backseat of the car.

"You'll make new friends," his mother said.

"What if it's no fun?" Tim continued.

"You'll have a great time, Tim," said his father as he wedged the sleeping bag into the already crowded car. "Trust us," he added.

Tim was worried. At first, going to camp seemed like a good idea. His best friend, Jeff, was going, too, and they had talked for hours about all the fun they would have together. Canoeing and archery were the activities that sounded like the most fun.

Then Jeff's grandmother got sick, and the whole Thompson family had to change their summer plans. Jeff would have to miss camp.

"I'm just not sure I want to go to camp," Tim tried for the final time.

"Don't be such a doubting Thomas," his mother said with a smile. "By this time next week, you probably won't even want to come home."

Discuss

1. Why did Tim's mother call him a doubting Thomas?

2. Have you ever been a doubting Thomas? When?

Activity

Tim had to trust his parents about going to camp. Finish the
letter below that Tim wrote to his family from camp.

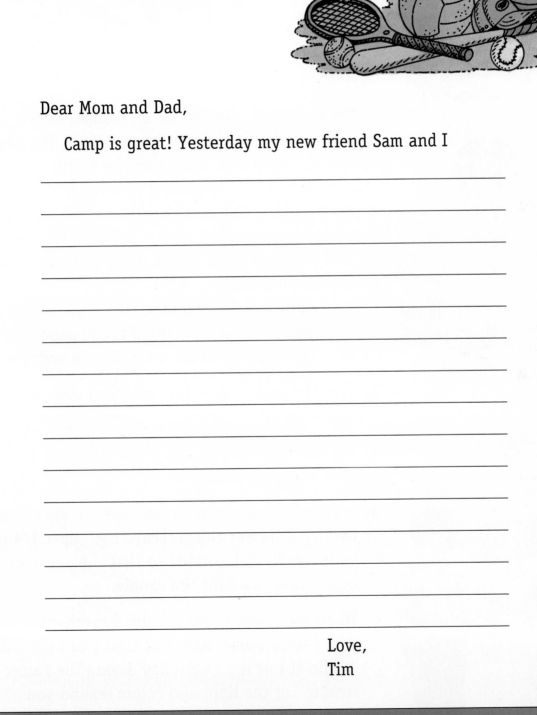

Dear Mom and Dad,

    Camp is great! Yesterday my new friend Sam and I

_____

_____

_____

_____

_____

_____

_____

_____

_____

_____

_____

                          Love,
                          Tim

An Easter Candle

For Catholic's, candles are a reminder of the presence of the risen Christ in our midst. The Easter candle in your parish church will be lighted each time the parish community gathers to worship during the Easter season and at every Baptism and funeral Mass throughout the year.

You will need these materials to make an Easter candle for your family.

- a white candle, any diameter
- scraps of different colored tissue paper
- a dish with equal amounts of glue and water

1. Tear the tissue paper into pieces of different shapes and sizes.

2. Dip the tissue paper, one piece at a time, into the glue mixture, soaking it well.

3. Put the wet pieces of tissue paper on your candle. Overlap different colors. Leave the upper 1/4 of your candle undecorated so that the paper will not burn when you light the candle.

4. When the tissue paper has dried thoroughly, take your candle home. Ask your family to light the candle at one meal each day during the Easter season. Let the light and colors remind you of the risen Jesus.

An Easter Prayer Celebration

Teacher: Thomas found it hard to believe that Jesus had risen from the dead. Jesus knew the disciples would need time to see him and talk with him. Let us listen to two gospel stories about Jesus' appearances to his disciples after his resurrection.

Reader 1: Mary of Magdala, a friend of Jesus, was weeping beside the empty tomb. She turned and saw Jesus, but Mary thought he was the gardener. Then Jesus said, "Mary." When she heard him call her name, Mary recognized Jesus. She was filled with joy. Jesus told her to tell the other disciples that she had seen him. So off she went to share the good news.

Based on John 20:11–18

All: Jesus, we believe you are with us. You call each of us by name. Help us to share the good news.

Reader 2: One evening Peter and some of the other disciples decided to go fishing. All night they caught nothing. At dawn, a man standing on the shore called out to them. "Friends, have you caught anything?" They answered, "Not a thing!" He told them to throw the net over the other side of the boat. The net was soon filled with so many fish they could hardly haul it in. Then one of the disciples shouted, "It is the Lord!" Peter jumped into the water and swam ashore. When they all arrived on shore, Jesus shared with them a meal of bread and fish.

Based on John 21:1–14

All: Jesus, we believe you are with us. Help us to share your love with one another.

Our Church Honors Saints

Mother Elizabeth Ann Seton

Elizabeth Bayley Seton was born in New York City on August 28, 1774. Her mother died when she was very young, so Elizabeth was raised by her father. Elizabeth's family did not belong to the Catholic Church.

In 1794, Elizabeth married William Seton. They had five children. Then William became very ill. He went to Italy with his wife and oldest daughter in the hope that his health would improve. They lived with a kind Catholic family there. Soon William died. But Elizabeth stayed with the family and learned about the Catholic faith.

When Elizabeth returned to New York, she wanted to become a member of the Catholic Church. Her relatives and friends turned away from her because of her decision. Elizabeth was now a poor widow with five children to care for.

Soon Elizabeth was invited to start a school for girls in Maryland. Oher women joined her, and the group formed a community of Catholic sisters. They later became the first Sisters of Charity in the United States. They wrote textbooks and trained teachers for the classrooms. The group also visited the poor and the sick, and they cared for children who had no families.

Elizabeth died on January 4, 1821. But she left behind many parish schools like the one she began in Maryland. The community Elizabeth founded still carries on her work. In 1975, she was officially named a saint of the Church, the first person born in the United States to be named a saint. We celebrate her feast day on January 4.

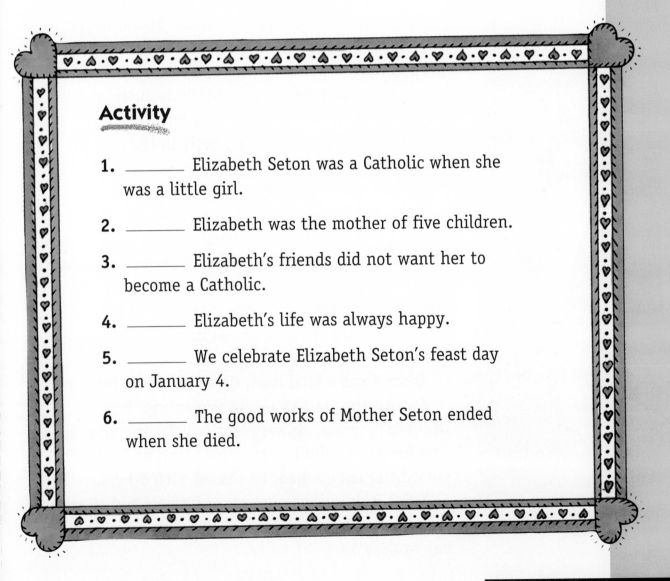

Activity

1. _____ Elizabeth Seton was a Catholic when she was a little girl.

2. _____ Elizabeth was the mother of five children.

3. _____ Elizabeth's friends did not want her to become a Catholic.

4. _____ Elizabeth's life was always happy.

5. _____ We celebrate Elizabeth Seton's feast day on January 4.

6. _____ The good works of Mother Seton ended when she died.

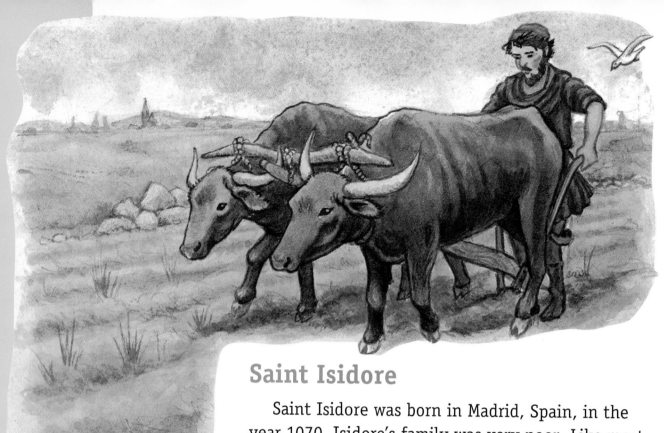

Saint Isidore

Saint Isidore was born in Madrid, Spain, in the year 1070. Isidore's family was very poor. Like most people, Isidore worked for another man who owned some land. The land around Madrid is dusty, red clay. The weather is dry and very hot. Each day, the workers would begin plowing early in the cool of the morning.

Isidore was a man of prayer. Early in the morning, he could be found in church, spending time with the Lord. Isidore would begin work several hours after the other workers. God seemed to reward Isidore for his prayerfulness. The stories about Saint Isidore tell of angels plowing alongside of him so that he was able to do twice as much work in half the time.

Isidore was a kind man. Often he would feed the birds with the corn he used for planting. Yet Isidore's crop was always plentiful. Other stories tell how he was careful not to harm a nest of field mice. What little Isidore had, he shared with others.

Saint Isidore is the patron of farmers and all who earn a living from the land. We celebrate his feast day on May 15.

Activity

The pictures below show farmers today. Study the pictures. Then on the lines below, tell in what ways it might be difficult for a Christian to be a farmer and in what ways it might be easy.

_____

_____

_____

_____

_____

_____

_____

_____

Saint Vincent de Paul

Vincent came from a poor farming family in France. In Vincent's time, most children began to work in the fields as soon as they were old enough. But Vincent's parents saw that he was very bright. They wanted him to get an education. They sacrificed to send Vincent to school. When Vincent finished his studies, he decided to become a priest.

Vincent's first "parish" was the royal court. He had an easy life, tutoring children and living in comfort. One day, something happened that changed Vincent's life. He visited a dying man who wanted to receive the sacrament of Reconciliation. Vincent was shocked at how poor the man was.

Vincent realized that the poor people of France needed help. They were hungry and they dressed in rags. They did not know God because no one cared enough about them to tell them how much God loved them. Vincent understood that this was the work God wanted him to do.

Vincent helped homeless children he found on the street. He organized groups in parishes to serve the poor. He began an order of priests, the Vincentians, to help fight against poverty.

Vincent met a woman named Louise de Marillac. They formed the Daughters of Charity, a community of religious women who nursed the sick and cared for orphans.

Vincent saw Jesus in the people he served. He reached out in love to people of all ages. He helped convicts and slaves. He sent priests to foreign lands to share God's word and to help anyone in need.

Vincent's work continues today. The Vincentian Fathers and the Daughters of Charity still care for others. Many parishes have Saint Vincent de Paul Societies that collect clothes, money, and food for the poor, homeless, and forgotten people of our world.

We honor Saint Vincent de Paul on September 27. Saint Vincent teaches us to follow Jesus' command: "Love your neighbor as yourself."

Activity

Find out about a group in your parish that serves those in need. Fill in the information you learn about the group in the space below.

What is the name of the group?

_____

Whom does the group serve?

_____

_____

_____

_____

How can you help?

_____

_____

_____

_____

Saint Agnes

"Look at this!" exclaimed Todd. "Saint Raymond of Penyafort lived to be one hundred years old!"

"And Saint Francis of Paola was ninety-one when he died," added Lisa.

"This book says there was a Saint Anthony who was one hundred five!" exclaimed Nick.

The fourth graders were helping Sister Agnes sort library books.

"Why does a person have to be old to be a saint?" asked Lisa.

"A person doesn't have to be old to be a saint," replied Sister.

"Can kids be saints?" Nick joined in.

"They certainly can," said Sister. "Let me tell you about a saint who was only a little older than you."

"The stories tell us," Sister began, "that this saint was only about twelve or thirteen when she died. She was very kind. From the time she was a little girl she wanted to belong completely to God.

"Many of the young men wanted to marry her, and when she refused, some of them became angry and jealous. This young girl lived at a time when it was dangerous to be known as a Christian. So one of the angry young men told the emperor that she was a Christian, and the emperor had her killed. Because this young girl was so good and kind and brave, we call her a saint."

"What was her name?" asked Todd.

"And why do you know so much about her?" questioned Lisa.

"Her name was Agnes," Sister Agnes answered with a smile.

"This is a statue of Saint Agnes that I received the day I became a religious sister. She is my patron saint, and her feast day is January 21."

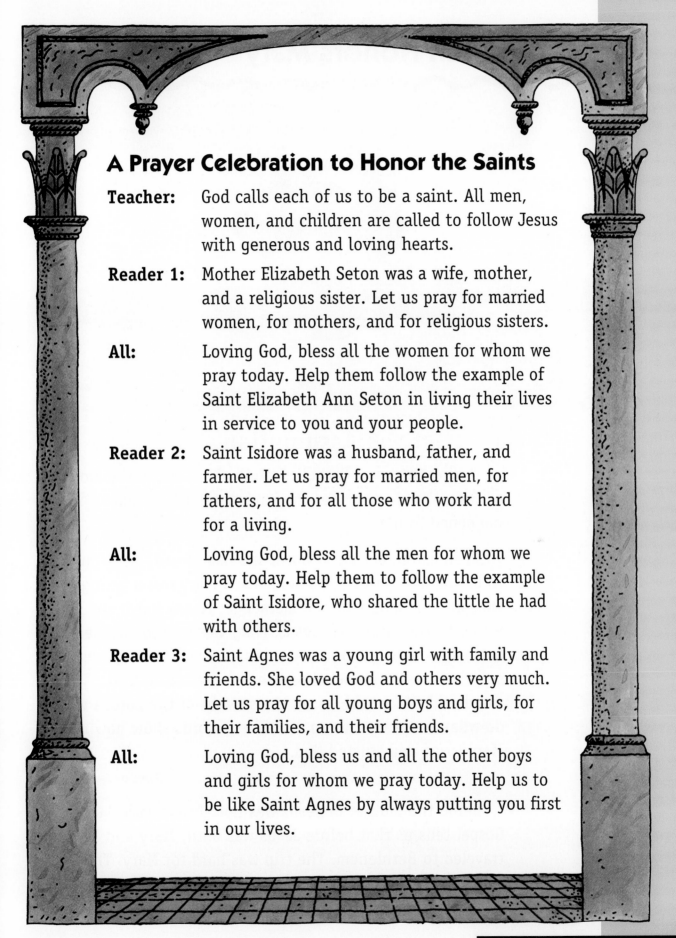

A Prayer Celebration to Honor the Saints

Teacher: God calls each of us to be a saint. All men, women, and children are called to follow Jesus with generous and loving hearts.

Reader 1: Mother Elizabeth Seton was a wife, mother, and a religious sister. Let us pray for married women, for mothers, and for religious sisters.

All: Loving God, bless all the women for whom we pray today. Help them follow the example of Saint Elizabeth Ann Seton in living their lives in service to you and your people.

Reader 2: Saint Isidore was a husband, father, and farmer. Let us pray for married men, for fathers, and for all those who work hard for a living.

All: Loving God, bless all the men for whom we pray today. Help them to follow the example of Saint Isidore, who shared the little he had with others.

Reader 3: Saint Agnes was a young girl with family and friends. She loved God and others very much. Let us pray for all young boys and girls, for their families, and their friends.

All: Loving God, bless us and all the other boys and girls for whom we pray today. Help us to be like Saint Agnes by always putting you first in our lives.

Our Church Honors Mary

Feast of the Assumption

During the year, Catholics think about Mary, the mother of Jesus. They remember the important things that happened to her.

Even before Mary was born, she had already been chosen to be the mother of God's Son. When Mary was a young woman, God sent a special messenger to ask her if she would be the mother of Jesus. Mary was free to choose between saying yes or no to God's messenger. Mary was surprised that God had chosen her for something so wonderful. Mary said, "I am the servant of the Lord. I will do what God wants me to do." These words show how much Mary loved and trusted God.

Based on Luke 1:26–38

Being the mother of Jesus was not always easy. Luke's Gospel tells us that before Jesus was born, Mary and Joseph traveled to Bethlehem. The trip was hard for Mary. Then, when Jesus was twelve years old, Joseph and Mary took him to the Temple in Jerusalem. He was lost there for three days. Mary was very worried about Jesus until he was found. In John's Gospel we read that when Jesus was crucified, Mary stayed near the cross until her son died.

We are not sure how long Mary lived after Jesus' resurrection. But we do believe that, when the time was right, Jesus brought his mother to heaven to be with God in glory. We say that Mary was assumed, or taken up into heaven, body and spirit.

On August 15 we celebrate the Feast of the Assumption. On that day we think about what Jesus did for his mother, Mary. We are happy because we know that we, too, will be with them in heaven someday.

Activity

To find the hidden message, cross out all the X's. Then copy the letters that are left on the lines to discover what Mary said to God's special messenger. We can say it, too.

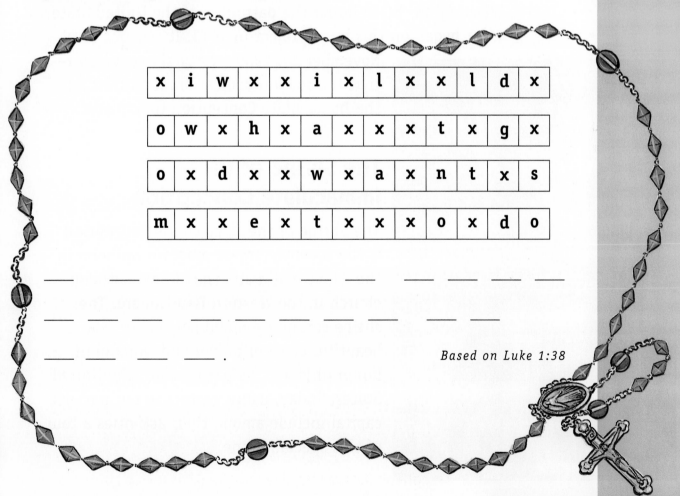

x	i	w	x	x	i	x	l	x	x	l	d	x

o	w	x	h	x	a	x	x	x	t	x	g	x

o	x	d	x	x	w	x	a	x	n	t	x	s

m	x	x	e	x	t	x	x	x	o	x	d	o

___ ___ ___ ___ ___ ___ ___ ___ ___

___ ___ ___ ___ ___ ___ ___ ___

___ ___ ___ ___ .

Based on Luke 1:38

Patroness of the Americas

Mary, the Mother of God, has been honored by the people of America from our earliest days. Christopher Columbus called one of his ships the *Santa Maria*, which means "Saint Mary." And many of the early cities and churches in the New World were named after Mary by the early explorers.

In 1846, the bishops of the United States wrote to Pope Pius IX to tell him they wished to choose Mary as the patroness of their country under the title of the Immaculate Conception. Pope Pius IX granted their request the following year.

In 1854, Pope Pius IX declared publicly and solemnly that from the first moment of her life, God kept Mary free from all sin. Catholics celebrate this belief each year on December 8, the Feast of the Immaculate Conception.

It was later decided to build a national shrine in Washington, DC to honor the patroness of the United States. Work began on this huge project in 1913. It was not until November 20, 1959—forty-six years later—that the solemn dedication of the Shrine of the Immaculate Conception took place.

The Shrine of the Immaculate Conception

The Shrine of the Immaculate Conception is the seventh largest religious building in the whole world and the largest Catholic church in the Western Hemisphere. The shrine can house 6,000 persons. It is a beautiful place of prayer and worship in honor of Mary, the patroness of the United States. Today, many visitors to our nation's capital include among their activities a tour of this special shrine.

Activity

Think about our country. What are some problems we face? Who are some people in the United Sates who need special help? Write a prayer, asking Mary, our patroness, to help us.

_____

_____

_____

_____

_____

_____

_____

_____

Millet's "The Angelus" from Musee d'Orsay, Paris

The Angelus

The Angelus is an ancient prayer that honors Mary as the mother of Jesus. In Latin, the word *angelus* means "angel." Latin was the official language of the Church for hundreds of years. The prayer is called "The Angelus" because it begins with the words, "The angel."

Long ago, monks prayed the Angelus three times a day: 6 A.M., noon, and 6 P.M. A bell called the monks to prayer. When they were out in the fields caring for the crops or the animals, the monks stopped working when they heard the bell ring. They knelt in the fields, or wherever they were working, and prayed the Angelus.

The Angelus is made up of verses from the Bible that are recited. When we pray the Angelus aloud, the group takes turns reciting the verses. After each verse, the Hail Mary is prayed.

The Angelus

The angel spoke God's message to Mary,
    and she conceived of the Holy Spirit.
Hail Mary, full of grace. . .
"I am the lowly servant of the Lord:
    Let it be done to me according to your word."
Hail Mary, full of grace. . .
And the Word became flesh,
    and lived among us.
Hail Mary, full of grace. . .
Pray for us, holy Mother of God,
    that we may become worthy of the promises
    of Christ.
Let us pray.
Lord, fill our hearts with your grace. Once, through the message of an angel, you revealed the Incarnation of Your Son; now, through his suffering and death, lead us to the glory of his resurrection. We ask this through Christ our Lord. Amen.

Activity

Working with a partner, look up the Scripture passages on the left. Match them with the verses from the Angelus on the right.

1. Luke 1:38

_____ The angel spoke God's message to Mary, and she conceived of the Holy Spirit.

2. John 1:14

_____ "I am the lowly servant of the Lord: Let it be done to me according to your word."

3. Luke 1:28–36

_____ And the Word became flesh, and lived among us.

Our Church Celebrates Holy Days

The Ascension of the Lord

After rising from the dead, Jesus appeared to his disciples for forty days. Jesus spoke to them about the kingdom of God. He told them to stay in Jerusalem to wait for the Spirit whom the Father promised to send. He said, "You will receive power when the Holy Spirit comes upon you. You will be my witnesses all over the earth."

After Jesus said this, and while they were watching, he was lifted up. A cloud took him out of their sight. The disciples could not see him, but as he went up, they kept looking up into the sky.

Suddenly, two men dressed in white clothing stood before them. They said, "Why are you standing there looking up into the sky? Jesus has been taken up into heaven. But he will return to you in the same way that you have seen him go."

Based on Acts of the Apostles 1:3–5, 8–11

Forty days after Easter, the Church celebrates the Feast of the Ascension. On this day, we remember that the risen Jesus returned to his Father in heaven. Before Jesus was taken up into heaven, he promised his followers that he would be with them always through the Holy Spirit that he promised God would send.

The ascension of Jesus is a wonderful sign to all of Jesus' followers. It tells us that if we try to live by Jesus' teachings and example, we, too, will one day share new life in God's heavenly kingdom.

One day, Jesus will return to us. On that day, he will announce that God's kingdom has been completed. Jesus will gather his followers together and welcome us into the kingdom, where perfect peace, love, and justice will rule. Jesus said, "I will see you again. Then your hearts will rejoice. No one will be able to take away your joy"

(Based on John 16:22).

Activity

Complete the sentences by writing the missing words on the correct lines.

1. After his resurrection, Jesus talked to his followers about the _____ of God.

2. We call Jesus' being taken up into heaven the _____.

3. We celebrate the ascension _____ days after Easter.

4. Jesus' ascension means that we, too, will share Jesus' new life in _____.

5. One day Jesus will _____ to us.

Pentecost Sunday

After Jesus' ascension, the disciples stayed in Jerusalem, as Jesus asked them, to wait for the coming of the Holy Spirit. They stayed in a house with Mary and some of the other women. Every day, they prayed and waited together.

On the day of Pentecost, all of Jesus' followers were together in one place. Suddenly there was a noise from heaven, like the sound of a strong wind. It filled the house where they were living. Then they saw what looked like tongues of fire. A tongue came to rest on each of them. All the disciples were filled with the Holy Spirit. The Holy Spirit gave them the ability to speak in different languages.

Many religious Jews from every nation in the world were staying in Jerusalem. When they heard this sound, a crowd gathered. They were confused because they heard Jesus' followers speaking to them in their own languages. Amazed, they said, "Aren't all these people from Galilee? How can each of us hear them speaking in our own language? We are from Judea, Asia, Egypt, and Rome and we hear them speaking in our own languages and telling the wonderful things God has done."

Based on Acts of the Apostles 2:1–11

The Church Celebrates the Holy Spirit

The Church celebrates Pentecost fifty days after Easter. On Pentecost, the Holy Spirit filled Jesus' followers with the courage to tell others the good news about Jesus. With the Spirit's help, Jesus' followers were able to carry on the work that Jesus had given them: "Go to the people of all nations and make them my disciples. Baptize them in the name of the Father, the Son, and the Holy Spirit, and teach them to do everything that I have told you" (based on Matthew 28:19–20).

We first receive the Holy Spirit at Baptism. In the sacrament of Confirmation, the gifts of the Spirit are strengthened within us. The Holy Spirit is the presence of Jesus. Through the Holy Spirit, Jesus is always with us. The Spirit is our helper and guide. The Holy Spirit helps us turn away from temptation and make good choices. Like Jesus' first followers, the Spirit helps us tell others the good news about Jesus and the kingdom of God.

Activity

Write a prayer to the Holy Spirit. Ask the Spirit to come into your life in a special way.

_____

_____

_____

_____

_____

_____

_____

_____

Feast of Saints Peter and Paul

On June 29, the Church celebrates the feast of two apostles and martyrs, Saints Peter and Paul.

Saint Peter's real name was Simon. Most of what we know about him, we learn from the Bible. The Bible tells us that Simon, like his brother Andrew, was a fisherman. Jesus saw them one day and invited them to follow him. From that day on, they followed Jesus and lived as Jesus lived.

We also learn how Jesus chose Simon to be the leader of the Apostles and the leader of his Church. Jesus said, "You are 'Rock,' and on this rock I will build my church (based on Matthew 16:18)." Simon's name was changed to Peter or Simon Peter, because the name *Peter* means "rock."

And we read in the Bible that Peter was afraid when Jesus was about to be put to death. He had said that he was not a friend of Jesus. But in the days after Jesus' death and resurrection, Peter was given a chance to tell Jesus how much he loved him. Later, Peter traveled to Rome to teach others how to follow Jesus. People who did not believe Peter's words crucified him there.

Saint Paul's name in Hebrew was Saul. Saul probably never met Jesus when Jesus was on earth. At first, Saul and his friends did not like Jesus' disciples. They wanted to find these people and have them punished. One day, as they traveled along, a light from the sky suddenly appeared. The group heard a voice. It was Jesus' voice. Jesus told Saul to stop speaking against him and to begin teaching the people that Jesus is the Son of God.

Saul, who used the Greek form of his name–Paul–traveled to faraway places to tell people about the risen Jesus. He kept in touch with these people by writing letters. We hear these letters read to us at Mass. They tell us how to be followers of Jesus.

Activity

Complete the sentences by filling in the missing words.

1. The new name Jesus gave to a fisherman was _____.

2. After Jesus' resurrection, Peter told Jesus that he _____ him.

3. Peter died on a _____ like Jesus.

4. Later in his life, Saul took the name _____.

5. Paul's letters teach us how to _____ Jesus.

In the Spirit of Jesus

Pope John Paul II

When Karol Wojtyla was in college, the people of his country were living in fear. The German army had attacked Poland. Schools were closed and Karol had to go to work. During the war, Karol became angry at the injustices he saw. He wanted to speak out against the way people were being treated. Karol felt that God was calling him to a life of service. He decided to become a priest.

Karol was ordained a year after the war ended. Father Wojtyla loved being a parish priest. He was a wonderful preacher who shared Jesus' message of hope and love with his people. When he was only thirty-eight, he became a bishop. Soon after, he was named Cardinal of Krakow, Poland. He spoke out for freedom and justice. He fought against Communism, which did not permit people to celebrate their faith. Some people hated Cardinal Wojtyla for talking about the rights of people. They warned him to stop.

In 1978, Karol Wojtyla became Pope John Paul II, the leader of the Catholic Church. John Paul II traveled all over the world, more than any other pope. He spoke out for equality. He repeated Jesus' message everywhere he went: "Love one another. We are all brothers and sisters. We must live in peace."

On May 13, 1981, while blessing the people in St. Peter's Square in Rome, Pope John Paul II was shot. He was rushed to the hospital for surgery. Four days later, the pope broadcast a message from his bed to the crowds in St. Peter's Square. He said that he was praying for the man who shot him. He called the man "his brother." After he had recovered, John Paul II visited the jail where the would-be assassin was being held. He prayed with the man who tried to kill him. The pope forgave him and blessed him.

Pope John Paul II is a living example of the peace and reconciliation Jesus came to bring. His life reminds us to treat every human being with love and respect and to forgive those who have hurt us.

Activity

If Pope John Paul II came to your city or town today, what do you think he would speak out against? What message would he have for you and your family? Write your ideas on the lines below.

_____

_____

_____

_____

_____

_____

_____

Sister Thea Bowman

Thea Bowman was born in Yazuu City, Mississippi in 1937. She was the granddaughter of a slave and the daughter of a doctor. Doctor Bowman, Thea's father, was not allowed to care for patients in the local hospital because the hospital was not open to African Americans.

Thea became a Catholic when she was twelve years old. She made this decision because she saw how much the nuns and priests loved Jesus and witnessed their work with the poor families in Thea's hometown. She was so impressed by their faith that Thea joined the convent when she was fifteen. She became a Franciscan Sister of Perpetual Adoration.

Sister Thea's life was a celebration. She shared the good news with children, teenagers, and college students. She sang, danced, told stories, and read poetry to help people of all ages understand God's love. She often prayed a simple three-word prayer: "Use me, Lord." Thea wanted God to help her use her gifts to bring more peace, love, and justice to the world. She wanted everyone to know that there was a place for people of every color in God's kingdom.

In 1984, Sister Thea became very ill. Although she was in pain, she continued to give speeches all over the country. She also recorded gospel songs, in which she shared her African American music with the world. Thea called on people to break down the walls that separated them and to see each person as a special gift from God. "Be Irish American, be Italian American, be Native American, be African American," Thea said, "but be one in Christ."

Before Thea died, a friend asked her what he should say at her funeral. Thea said, "Tell them that I'm going home like a shooting star." Sister Thea Bowman went home to God on March 30, 1990.

Use me, Lord

Activity

Like Sister Thea, we can pray, "Use me, Lord." We can ask God to help us use our talents to bring more peace, love, and justice to the world. On the lines below, write two talents or gifts that you have been given. Tell how these gifts can be used to help God's kingdom grow in the world.

_____

_____

_____

_____

Use me, Lord

Use me, Lord

Use me, Lord

Use me, Lord

OUR CATHOLIC HERITAGE

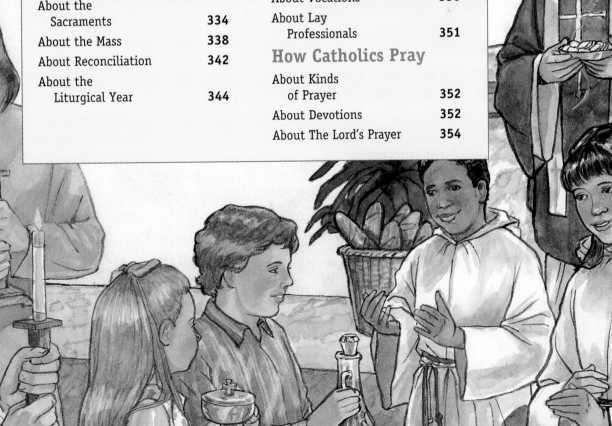

WHAT CATHOLICS BELIEVE

We can come to know and understand our faith in many ways.

ABOUT The Bible

The **Bible** is the story of God and God's people. It is the written word of God. The word *Bible* means "books." In the Bible there are seventy-three books of stories, laws, history, poetry, and prayers.

The Bible was the first book ever printed by machine. Today millions of Bibles are printed and read by people throughout the

world. The Bibles may have a different number of pages and may be written in different languages. However, all Bibles give us the same message of God.

To read the Bible more easily, we need to know how to find the parts or passages that are indicated in Bible references. Each time there is a passage from the Bible in your book, there is a Bible reference at the end. Finding passages in the Bible is not like finding something in a story book or a textbook. Remember, the Bible is made up of many books. Each book has a name. Each book is divided into chapters, and each chapter has a number. The chapters are divided into verses, which may contain one or more sentences. Verses also have numbers.

There is a Bible passage in this book on page 93. To find this passage in the Bible, you will need to find Sirach 6:14. Use the key to help you. Begin by finding the Book of Sirach (it is in the Old Testament). Then find Chapter 6. Finally, find verse 14.

Sirach	6:	14
Book	Chapter	Verse

Sometimes the Bible passage contains more than one verse. For example, in Matthew 9:1–8, you are reading verses one through eight.

The Holy Land

PHOENICIA

*Great Sea
(Mediterranean Sea)*

GALILEE

*Sea of
Galilee*

Nazareth

River Jordan

SAMARIA

PEREA

North

West — East

South

*Mount
of
Olives* Jericho

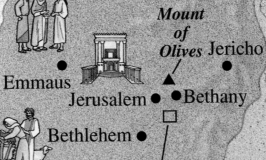

Emmaus

Jerusalem Bethany

Bethlehem

*Garden of
Gethsemani*

*Dead
Sea*

JUDEA

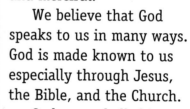The Trinity

We Believe in God

There is only one God. We know God as three Persons: God the Father, God the Son, and God the Holy Spirit. We believe that there is one God in three Persons, whom we call the **Blessed Trinity.**

God is all-good, all-holy, and all-knowing. God is always just and merciful.

We believe that God speaks to us in many ways. God is made known to us especially through Jesus, the Bible, and the Church.

God created all things out of goodness and love. Human beings are made in the image and likeness of God. We share the gift of God's life and loving presence as well as the responsibility to help care for the world.

We Believe in Jesus

Jesus, God's own Son, is the Second Person of the Blessed Trinity. Jesus is both God and man. Our belief that God became human in Jesus while remaining God is called the **Incarnation.** Jesus is both human and divine.

Jesus is the **Messiah,** sent by God. Jesus' mission was to announce the good news about God's reign of peace, love, and justice, to save us from sin, and to bring us everlasting life. Jesus taught, healed, forgave sins, and worked miracles to show us how much God loves us.

Jesus suffered and died to save all people from sin and death. Jesus is the **Savior** of the world, who saves us by his life, death, and **resurrection**.

Jesus rose to new life and invites us to share this new life with him. The resurrection fills us with hope. Jesus' resurrection teaches us that death is not an ending but rather a new beginning that leads us to new and everlasting life.

After the resurrection, Jesus shared his mission with the Apostles. He promised to send the Holy Spirit to be with them. Then Jesus returned in glory to his Father. Catholics call Jesus' return to God the **ascension**.

We Believe in the Holy Spirit

The **Holy Spirit** is the Third Person of the Blessed Trinity. The Holy Spirit is the love that is shared by the Father and the Son. The Spirit leads and guides us in living as followers of Jesus.

The Holy Spirit has been at work since Creation. With the help of the Spirit, the authors of the Bible wrote God's word. At **Pentecost**, the Holy Spirit gave the disciples the courage to share Jesus' good news. The Holy Spirit works in the Church today, helping us carry on Jesus' work. The Spirit works and lives in us. We are temples of the Holy Spirit.

ABOUT The Catholic Church

Catholics are followers of Jesus, and under the leadership of the pope and bishops, receive and share the Scriptures, worship God, celebrate the seven sacraments, and serve those in need.

The Church and her members are identified by four marks: one, holy, catholic, and apostolic.

The Church is **one**. We believe in one God—Father, Son, and Holy Spirit—one faith, and one Baptism. Our belief in Jesus unites us.

The Church is **holy**. God shares holiness with us. We are called to become holy and be filled with God's goodness.

The Church is **catholic**, or universal. The Catholic Church welcomes all people.

The Church is **apostolic**. The truths of our faith and our way of life come down to us from the Apostles.

The chief teacher of the Church is the pope. We believe that the pope represents Jesus on earth.

ABOUT Mary and the Saints

Catholics believe that Mary, the mother of Jesus, was born without original sin. This special gift from God is called the Immaculate Conception. From the first moment of life, Mary was filled with grace and lived a sinless life.

We honor Mary as mother of Jesus and mother of the Church. Mary is our mother, too. She loves and cares for us.

Catholics believe that Mary was taken up to heaven, body and soul, and shares in Jesus' resurrection. We call this belief Mary's assumption.

Mary is our greatest **saint**. Saints are special men and women who show us how to follow Jesus. We honor the saints and ask them to pray to God for us.

ABOUT Life Everlasting

We believe that one day Jesus will return in glory to announce that God's plan for the world is completed. We wait with hope for the time when God's perfect peace, love, and justice will be fulfilled when Christ comes again in glory. We work to bring God's kingdom to the world now.

Jesus teaches us that if we follow his example, we will be happy forever in heaven. Heaven is unending happiness with God and all who love God. If we have shown love for God, ourselves, and others, we will be together in heaven.

Those who have deliberately refused, in serious ways, to love God and their neighbor, and have not asked forgiveness, separate themselves forever from God and those who love God. We call this everlasting separation **hell**.

Catholics have a sacred history of **worship**. Worship is giving honor and praise to God. Through the sacraments and prayer, we praise, thank, adore, and ask God's help.

ABOUT The Sacraments

The **sacraments** are sacred signs that celebrate God's love for us and Jesus' presence in our lives and in the Church. There are seven sacraments. Through the sacraments, we are united with Jesus and share in God's life—grace.

The Sacraments of Initiation. We become full members of the Church through the three sacraments of initiation. The sacraments of initiation are Baptism, Confirmation, and Eucharist.

Baptism welcomes us into the Christian community, frees us from original sin and all sins, and unites us with Jesus.

During the celebration the priest or deacon pours water over the head of the person being baptized as he prays, "I baptize you in the name of the Father, and of the Son, and of the Holy Spirit (Rite of Baptism)."

We are born into a sinful condition that separates us from God. This condition is called **original sin**. Baptism frees us from original sin and all sins, and reunites us with God. We receive the Holy Spirit at Baptism.

Through the waters of Baptism, which represent life and death, we share in Jesus' death and resurrection. We are called away from sin to new life with Jesus.

Confirmation strengthens the new life we received at Baptism and makes us living witnesses of Jesus in the world.

During the celebration the bishop or priest lays his hand on the head of the one to be confirmed and anoints the forehead with chrism as he prays, "Be sealed with the Gift of the Holy Spirit (Rite of Confirmation)."

Confirmation is usually celebrated with a bishop. The Holy Spirit gives us special gifts to help us share Jesus' good news by our words and actions.

Eucharist celebrates the real presence of Jesus' Body and Blood under the appearances of bread and wine.

During the celebration the priest prays the words of consecration over the bread and wine, which become the body and blood of Christ.

The Eucharist is our greatest act of worship. At the Last Supper, Jesus gave us his body and blood so that we could live forever.

The Eucharist makes Jesus' sacrifice on the cross and his resurrection from the dead present for us. The word *Eucharist* means "thanksgiving." During the Mass we praise and thank God for all our gifts, especially the gift of Jesus.

Jesus is truly present in the Eucharist. The bread and wine still have the appearance of ordinary bread and wine, but through the power of the Holy Spirit, they become Jesus' Body and Blood.

The Eucharist unites us with Jesus and the Church community. Jesus is also present in the people gathered to celebrate the Eucharist, in the word proclaimed, and in the priest who presides.

The Sacraments of Healing

In the sacraments of healing—Reconciliation and Anointing of the Sick—we celebrate Jesus' forgiveness and healing.

Reconciliation celebrates God's healing and forgiveness of our sins. During the celebration the priest prays the prayer of absolution, ending with the words, "I absolve you from your sins in the name of the Father, and of the Son, and of the Holy Spirit (Rite of Penance).

When we sin, we freely choose to turn away from God and one another. Reconciliation reunites us with God and the Church community. In the sacrament of Reconciliation, the priest represents the loving forgiveness of God and the Church. We may celebrate the sacrament of Reconciliation whenever we need God's mercy and peace. We may celebrate the sacrament individually or communally.

Anointing of the Sick brings Jesus' healing, comfort, and strength to those who are seriously ill, elderly, or in danger of death.

During the celebration, the priest anoints the person with the oil of the sick as he prays, "Through this holy anointing may the Lord in his love and mercy help you with the grace of the Holy Spirit. May the Lord who frees you from sin save you and raise you up" (Rite of Anointing).

Before the anointing, the sick may celebrate Reconciliation. The Eucharist may be received after the anointing.

We can help people who are old or sick by praying for them, visiting them, and helping them in any way we can.

The Sacraments of Commitment

In the sacraments of commitment, the Church celebrates two special ways through which people serve others by sharing their gifts. The sacraments of commitment are Matrimony and Holy Orders.

Matrimony celebrates the lifelong love of a man and a woman for each other. During the celebration, the bride and groom exchange marriage vows, promising always to be faithful to each other.

Through Matrimony the couple forms a partnership based on love. The man and woman promise to love each other in sickness and in health. They promise to be faithful to each other. Their love for each other is a sign of God's love for all people.

In **Holy Orders** bishops, priests, and deacons are ordained to serve the Church in a special way.

During the celebration, the bishop lays his hands on the head of the person to be ordained. Afterwards, he prays a prayer of consecration, or blessing.

Bishops, priests, and deacons are blessed to share in Jesus' ministry in a special way. Bishops carry on the work of the Apostles and lead dioceses. Bishops teach and serve the Catholic Church. Priests help the bishop in his ministry. Priests, like bishops, celebrate the sacraments, proclaim God's word, and help us become better signs of his kingdom. Deacons care for the poor and do other works of mercy. They may baptize, proclaim the gospel, witness marriages, and preside at funerals.

ABOUT The Mass

Introductory Rites

At Mass we come together to pray and worship as the family of Jesus.

Entrance Procession and Gathering Song

As the priest and other ministers enter in procession, we stand and sing a gathering song.

Greeting

We make the sign of the cross. The priest welcomes us by saying, "The Lord be with you." We answer, "And also with you."

Penitential Rite

As a community, we admit that we have sinned and we thank God for his gift of forgiveness. We pray the opening prayer.

Gloria

We sing or say this hymn of praise to God.

Liturgy of the Word

First Reading

The lector reads from the Old Testament or the Acts of the Apostles about God's love for us.

Responsorial Psalm

The song leader sings a psalm from the Bible. We join in singing a response.

Second Reading

The lector reads from the New Testament, usually from one of the letters.

Gospel Acclamation

Before the gospel is proclaimed by the priest or deacon, we sing, "Alleluia" or another acclamation.

Gospel

We stand in honor of Jesus as the gospel is proclaimed.

Homily

The priest or deacon explains the readings, especially the gospel, in a special talk called the homily.

Profession of Faith

We stand to declare our beliefs by reciting the Nicene Creed.

General Intercessions

We pray for the pope and the bishops, for our country, and for all God's people.

Liturgy of the Eucharist

Preparation of the Altar and the Gifts

We bring gifts of bread and wine to the altar as the table is prepared for the meal we are about to share.

Eucharistic Prayer

In this prayer of praise and thanksgiving, the priest addresses God our Father in our name. Together we sing a song of praise to God for his many blessings, especially for the gift of Jesus.

"Holy, holy, holy Lord, God of power and might. Heaven and earth are full of your glory. Hosanna in the highest. Blessed is he who comes in the name of the Lord. Hosanna in the highest."

Together with the priest, we call upon the Holy Spirit and ask that the bread and wine become Jesus' Body and Blood. The priest consecrates the bread and wine. We proclaim the mystery of faith. We sing or say these or other words of joy and praise, "Christ has died, Christ is risen, Christ will come again."

As the Eucharistic Prayer ends, we proclaim, "Amen."

Communion Rite

The Lord's Prayer

We pray together the prayer that Jesus taught us—The Lord's Prayer.

Sign of Peace

We offer each other a sign of peace to show that we are all brothers and sisters in Jesus.

Breaking of the Bread

While the priest breaks the host, we sing or say,

"Lamb of God, you take away the sins of the world, have mercy on us.

Lamb of God, you take away the sins of the world, have mercy on us.

Lamb of God, you take away the sins of the world, grant us peace."

Communion

Jesus invites us to receive the Eucharist.

Concluding Rite

Blessing

The priest blesses us in the name of God the Father, God the Son, and God the Holy Spirit. We answer, "Amen."

Dismissal

The priest tells us to go in peace to love and serve God and others. We sing a song of thanks and praise.

ABOUT Reconciliation

The sacrament of Reconciliation, or Penance, celebrates God's love and forgiveness through the Church.

Preparation   I prepare myself for the sacrament of Reconciliation by thinking about my words and actions. This is called an examination of conscience. How do I fulfill God's commands to love him and to love my neighbor as myself? Am I sorry for having sinned?

Rite for Reconciliation of Individuals

Priest's Welcome   The priest welcomes me in the name of Jesus and the Church.

Reading from Scripture   The priest may share with me a reading from the Bible.

Confession   I tell my sins to the priest. This is called my confession. He then suggests ways in which I might grow closer to God and asks me to say a prayer or do a kind act to help make up for my sins. This is called an act of penance.

Prayer of Sorrow   The priest then asks me to tell God that I am sorry for my sins. I say an act of contrition.

Absolution   Acting in the name of the Christian community, the priest extends his hands over me and asks God to forgive me. The priest forgives me in the name of the Father, the Son, and the Holy Spirit. This is called absolution.

Prayer of Praise and Dismissal   After receiving absolution, I praise God with the priest. He says, "The Lord has freed you from your sins. Go in peace." I answer, "Amen."

Celebrating Reconciliation in Community

Sometimes we gather as a community to celebrate the sacrament of Reconciliation.

Introductory Rites   We sing an opening hymn. The priest greets us and invites us to pray for God's forgiveness.

Celebration of the Word of God   We listen to readings from the Bible. The priest reads the gospel and gives a homily.

Examination of Conscience   We examine our conscience and tell God we are sorry for our sins.

Rite of Reconciliation   Together we pray an act of contrition and sing or say The Lord's Prayer. Then, one by one, we tell our sins to a priest and receive absolution.

Proclamation of Praise for God's Mercy   When individual confessions are completed, the priest invites us to praise and thank God for his mercy.

Concluding Rites   The priest then blesses us. We sing a song of praise and thanksgiving.

ABOUT The Liturgical Year

The **liturgical year** is the Church's official calendar of feasts and seasons. It celebrates all the important events of Jesus' life and Jesus' presence with us today.

The Church year begins with **Advent**. Advent is a season of joyful waiting. We prepare to celebrate the birth of Jesus at Christmas.

During the Christmas season, we celebrate Jesus' birth. We also celebrate the Epiphany and the Baptism of Jesus.

Another major season of the Church year is **Lent**. During the forty days of Lent we prepare to celebrate Easter. It is a time of prayer and sacrifice. The last week of Lent is called Holy Week. On the first day of Holy Week we celebrate Passion Sunday (Palm Sunday), when we recall Jesus' triumphant entry into Jerusalem.

The last three days of Holy Week are known as the **Easter Triduum** — the holiest days of the liturgical year. On Holy Thursday, we remember the Last Supper. On Good Friday, we remember Jesus' crucifixion. On Holy Saturday evening, at a special liturgy called the Easter Vigil, we celebrate Jesus' resurrection. We continue this celebration on the following day, Easter Sunday — the Church's greatest feast.

The Easter season lasts for fifty days. During this time we celebrate the ascension of Jesus and the coming of the Holy Spirit on **Pentecost.**

During the Church year we also have a season called Ordinary Time. During this season, we celebrate all that Jesus has taught us. We listen to the stories of his life proclaimed in the gospel readings at Mass.

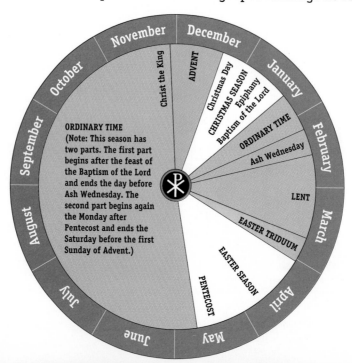

HOW CATHOLICS LIVE

The teachings of Jesus and the Church show us how Catholics live happy and loving lives.

ABOUT The Beatitudes

The Beatitudes are Jesus' teachings on how to find everlasting happiness. They teach us to love God and others, and promise us a place in the kingdom of heaven. Christians believe that they will be happy forever if they live the Beatitudes.

The Beatitudes	How We Live the Beatitudes
Happy are the poor in spirit. The reign of God is theirs.	We are poor in spirit when we know that we need God more than anything else in life.
Happy are the sorrowing. They will be comforted.	We obey God and trust in his goodness. We try to help those who are hurting. We know that God is with them.
Happy are the gentle. They will receive all that God has promised.	We are kind and loving. We use the gifts that God has given us to help others.
Happy are those who hunger and thirst for justice. They will be satisfied.	We work to help God's kingdom begin to take root in this world. We share the things we have with those in need.
Happy are those who show mercy to others. They will receive mercy.	We forgive anyone who has hurt us. We accept others and are patient with them.
Happy are the single-hearted. They will see God.	We show our love for God by loving our neighbor.
Happy are the peacemakers. They will be called children of God.	We try to bring God's peace to the world. We help people make up after a fight.
Happy are those who are treated unfairly for doing what is right. The reign of God is theirs.	We carry on Jesus' work in the world. We stand up for what is right, even though it is not always easy.

ABOUT The Commandments

Jesus taught that it is important to obey the Ten Commandments.
The Commandments guide us in living as children of God.

The Ten Commandments	The Commandments Help Us to Live
1. I, the Lord, am your God. You shall not have other gods besides me.	We believe in and love God more than anyone or anything else in life. We remember God's gifts to us. We talk to and listen to God in prayer.
2. You shall not take the name of the Lord, your God, in vain.	We use the names of God, Jesus, and all holy persons, places, and things with respect and love. We never say God's or Jesus' name in anger.
3. Remember to keep holy the Sabbath day.	We worship God by celebrating the Eucharist together on Sunday. We relax and do special things on Sunday in honor of God.
4. Honor your father and mother.	We love, respect, and obey our parents and all adults who care for us.
5. You shall not kill.	We show respect for human life by caring for all people. We never fight or hurt others.
6. You shall not commit adultery.	We respect our bodies and the bodies of others. We use our sexuality according to God's plan.
7. You shall not steal.	We never take things that belong to someone else. We are careful with other people's things. We do not cheat.
8. You shall not bear false witness against your neighbor.	We are truthful and honest. We never tell lies or hurt others by what we say.
9. You shall not covet your neighbor's wife.	We respect the promises that married people have made to each other.
10. You shall not covet anything that belongs to your neighbor.	We are satisfied with what we have. We are not jealous or greedy.

The Great Commandment

"You shall love the Lord, your God, with all your heart, with all your being, with all your strength, and with all your mind, and your neighbor as yourself" (Luke 10:27).

Jesus summed up the Ten Commandments in the **Great Commandment**, which teaches us that God's laws are based on love of God and love of neighbor.

The New Commandment

"This is my commandment: love one another as I love you" (John 15:12).

Jesus' love is the perfect example of how to live. Our love for each other is a sign of Jesus' love.

ABOUT The Works of Mercy

Jesus teaches that when we serve others, we serve him. The loving acts described in Matthew 25:31–46 are called the **corporal** and **spiritual works of mercy**. The Works of Mercy tell us how to respond to the basic needs of all people.

The Corporal Works of Mercy

1. Feed the hungry.
2. Give drink to the thirsty.
3. Clothe the naked.
4. Visit those in prison.
5. Shelter the homeless.
6. Visit the sick.
7. Bury the dead.

The Spiritual Works of Mercy

1. Help others make good choices.
2. Teach those who lack knowledge.
3. Give advice to those who are confused.
4. Comfort those who are hurting.
5. Be patient with others.
6. Forgive injuries.
7. Pray for the living and the dead.

ABOUT Moral Living

Obstacles to Living a Moral Life

Sin keeps us from living as followers of Jesus. Sin is a free choice to turn away from God's love. We can sin by doing something we know is wrong, or we can sin by not doing what we know is right.

Mortal sin is a very serious refusal to live God's laws. Mortal sin turns us away from God and the Church community. However, even when we sin God's mercy and love never leave us.

There are three ways to tell if a sin is mortal.
- The action must be seriously wrong.
- We must know that the action is seriously wrong.
- We must make a free choice to commit the sin.

Mortal sins must be confessed in the sacrament of Reconciliation. Through Jesus, we receive God's mercy and forgiveness. We are reunited with God and the Church.

Less serious sins are called **venial sins**. Venial sins weaken but do not completely destroy our relationship with God and the Church community.

Helps in Living a Moral Life

Jesus calls us to live a **moral** life. We can live a moral life by following the teachings of Jesus and the Church. The Holy Spirit is always with us to help us make good moral decisions.

The Holy Spirit helps us turn away from sin and live as followers of Jesus. The Spirit guides our conscience—the ability to judge whether something is right or wrong. The Spirit helps us fight against temptation—a strong feeling that attracts us to do something wrong.

Catholics call God's loving presence in our lives *grace*. Grace gives us the strength to say no to selfishness and to act as the good people God created us to be. Grace helps us choose what is good.

ABOUT The Gifts of the Holy Spirit

The gifts of the Holy Spirit describe the ways the Spirit helps and guides us.

The Gifts of the Holy Spirit

1. **Wisdom** helps us know how God wants us to live.

2. **Understanding** helps us to be aware of all that God has taught us through Jesus, the Bible, and the Church.

3. **Knowledge** helps us to know that God is more important than anything else in life.

4. **Right Judgment** helps us make good decisions.

5. **Courage** helps us to be strong when faced with problems.

6. **Reverence** helps us to love God as our Father and to show our love in prayer.

7. **Wonder and Awe** help us to be filled with wonder and thanks for all that God creates.

Vocations

Many Ways of Serving

Lay Persons   Most Catholics live out their baptismal vocation as lay persons. Lay persons usually hold jobs in society and are either single or married. As part of their Christian vocation, lay persons often volunteer their time and skills in serving the local parish community, or even the local diocese. They may care for the poor, teach religious education classes, plan and lead the liturgy, help with parish organizations, or invite others to join the Church. In these and other ways, lay persons help the parish community fulfill its mission to reach out to all in the spirit of Jesus.

Vowed Religious   Some men and women choose to devote their entire lives to the ministry of the Catholic Church. These people join religious communities of sisters or brothers. Vows or promises of poverty, chastity, and obedience are taken so that the sisters or brothers can be completely devoted to their ministries and to becoming closer to God in community. Each religious community chooses particular ministries such as teaching, working with the poor, preaching, prayer and contemplation, nursing work, or parish work.

Ordained Ministers   In the Catholic Church, there are also ordained ministers — bishops, priests, and deacons. Baptized persons who are called to ordained ministry have the special vocation of leading the community in worship as well as serving in a wide variety of ministries within the Church.

Bishops are the chief teachers of the faith. They administer dioceses and celebrate the sacraments.

Diocesan priests serve in positions such as pastors of parishes, educators, and counselors. Priests who belong to religious communities may be assigned as pastors or teachers, or they may be assigned to the particular ministry of their communities.

Deacons   Most deacons are called permanent deacons. These men usually assist the pastor of a parish by leading the celebrations of Baptism and Marriage, preaching at Sunday Mass, and helping with parish management. Unlike priests, permanent deacons can be married and have families.

ABOUT The Lay Professionals

Some lay men and women called **lay professionals** choose to work full time in Church ministries. These Church leaders are more than lay volunteers. Lay professionals hold a full-time professional job within the Church community.

Lay professionals serve in various positions, such as Catholic school teachers or principals, directors of religious education in the parish or diocese, or as leaders of diocesan offices or organizations.

Other lay professionals help plan and direct the celebration of the Mass and the sacraments or act as pastoral associates. Still others dedicate their lives to youth ministry, hospital ministry, or ministry to the poor.

There are also many lay professionals who are missionaries in foreign countries. Missionaries help start Catholic communities in places where people may not have heard about God, Jesus, or the Church.

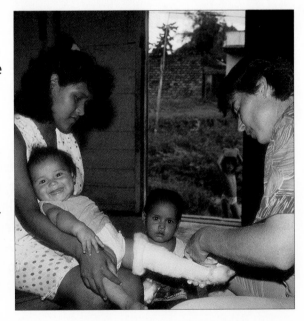

Lay professionals come from many different family backgrounds and bring many skills to their work in the Christian community. Together with bishops, priests, and religious women and men, lay professionals are Church leaders who help the Church grow into the community that Jesus asks us to be.

How Catholics Pray

Through prayer, Catholics show their love for God and ask God's help. The Church is united through the celebration of the sacraments and the prayers of all its members.

ABOUT Kinds of Prayer

Prayer is talking and listening to God. We can pray for the needs of others. We can make our whole life a prayer. We can greet God in the morning with prayer. We can pray before meals. We can thank God for our day before we go to sleep. God always hears our prayers.

Meditation is a way of praying without words. When we meditate, God speaks to us in our hearts. We can pray in this way by remembering a Bible story or by using our imagination to think of God, Jesus, the Holy Spirit, or Mary. As we pray, we can think about our friendship with God.

ABOUT Devotions

Sometimes we pray directly to God. Other times we express our love for God through our devotion to Mary, or the saints. We call these special prayers devotions.

The Rosary

Rosary means "garland of roses." When we pray the Rosary, we repeat the Hail Mary and other prayers over and over to praise Mary. At the same time we think about the most important events in the lives of Jesus and Mary, which we call *mysteries.*

The mysteries that name the events in Jesus' life help us to remember the things that Jesus did to bring justice and peace to the world. In this way, we come to know Jesus as the center of Mary's life and our lives.

The rosary has a crucifix, followed by one large bead and three small beads. Then there is a circle with five decades. Each decade is made up of The Lord's Prayer, followed by ten Hail Marys.

We begin the Rosary with the Sign of the Cross and the Apostles' Creed, The Lord's Prayer, three Hail Marys, and the Glory Be to the Father. We complete the Rosary by praying the five decades.

For each decade we pray The Lord's Prayer and ten Hail Marys, followed by the Glory Be to the Father. As we pray each decade, we think of the joyful, sorrowful, and glorious events in the lives of Jesus and Mary.

The Way of the Cross

The Way of the Cross, or Stations, is a traditional Catholic devotion most often prayed during the season of Lent. As we pray the Stations, we reflect on the passion, death, and resurrection of Jesus.

The Stations of the Cross

1. Jesus is condemned to death.
2. Jesus accepts the cross.
3. Jesus falls the first time.
4. Jesus meets his mother.
5. Simon helps Jesus carry the cross.
6. Veronica wipes the face of Jesus.
7. Jesus falls the second time.
8. Jesus meets the women of Jerusalem.
9. Jesus falls the third time.
10. Jesus is stripped of his garments.
11. Jesus is nailed to the cross.
12. Jesus dies on the cross.
13. Jesus is taken down from the cross.
14. Jesus is buried in the tomb.
15. Jesus rises from the dead.

ABOUT The Lord's Prayer

Jesus taught his followers to pray. We call the prayer of Jesus **The Lord's Prayer**. In this special prayer, we honor God and ask his help.

Our Father, who art in heaven, **hallowed** *be thy name.*
God is our Father. We pray that everyone will remember how good God is.

Thy kingdom come,
Jesus told us about God's kingdom. We pray that everyone will live as Jesus taught us to live.

thy will be done on earth as it is in heaven.
We pray that everyone will obey God's laws.

Give us this day our daily bread;
We know that God cares for us. We pray for our needs and the needs of the poor.

and forgive us our trespasses as we forgive those who trespass against us;
We ask God to forgive us for the wrong things we have done.

and lead us not into temptation,
We ask God to help us always to choose what is right.

but deliver us from evil.
We pray that God will protect us from things that may harm us.

Amen.
Our *Amen* means "Let it be."

absolution

the prayer of forgiveness prayed by the priest in the sacrament of Reconciliation *(page 217)*

abuse

violence toward someone or something *(page 139)*

adultery

being unfaithful to one's husband or wife by giving to someone else the special love promised in marriage *(page 145)*

Advent

four weeks of preparation before Christmas *(page 344)*

Anointing of the Sick

the sacrament of healing that brings Jesus' healing, comfort, and strength to those who are seriously ill, elderly, or in danger of death *(page 336)*

apostolic

one of the four marks, or qualities, of the Church that show its truth and its origin in God. The Church is apostolic, founded on and faithful to the Apostles' teachings *(page 332)*

ascension

the returning of Jesus in glory to his Father *(page 331)*

assumption

the taking up of Mary, body and soul, to heaven *(page 333)*

Baptism

the first sacrament of initiation, through which we are freed of original sin and welcomed into the Church *(page 334)*

bear false witness

to tell a lie *(page 175)*

Beatitudes

the teachings of Jesus on how to live happily; how Jesus lived *(page 75)*

Bible

the story of God and God's people; the written word of God *(page 328)*

Blessed Trinity

one God in three Persons *(page 330)*

catholic

one of the four marks, or qualities, of the Church that show its truth and its origin in God. The Church is catholic, or universal, open to all people *(page 332)*

Catholic Church

the Christian community which celebrates the seven sacraments and recognizes the pope and bishops as its leaders *(page 223)*

cheat

to get something from someone in a dishonest way *(page 165)*

commandment

a law given to us by God to help us live good lives by being loving people *(page 63)*

compassion
feeling another's pain and wanting to relieve it *(page 195)*

Confirmation
a sacrament of initiation in which we become fuller members of the Church and in which the Holy Spirit makes us stronger to live and share our faith in Jesus *(page 335)*

conscience
our power to judge whether something is good or bad *(page 43)*

consequences
the things that follow from a choice or an action *(page 25)*

Corinthians
the people who lived in Corinth, a city in Greece *(page 225)*

covet
to want something someone else has *(page 145)*

disciples
followers of Jesus *(page 83)*

Easter Triduum
the three holiest days of the year. On Holy Thursday, we remember the Last Supper; on Good Friday, we remember Jesus' crucifixion; on Holy Saturday, at the Easter Vigil, we celebrate Jesus' resurrection *(page 344)*

envy
wanting something that belongs to another *(page 163)*

Eucharist
a sacrament of initiation and of unity and love in which we receive the body and blood of Jesus *(page 335)*

examination of conscience
thinking about what we have said and done and how we may have sinned *(page 215)*

faithful
able to be trusted and depended upon *(page 143)*

Galilean
someone from Galilee, the land north of Samaria *(page 193)*

grace
God's loving presence in our lives *(page 17)*

Great Commandment, the
the commandment in which Jesus summed up the Ten Commandments by teaching us that God's laws are based on love of God and love of neighbor *(page 347)*

greed
wanting more and more things when they are not needed *(page 163)*

heaven
being with God forever *(page 95)*

hell
eternal separation from God and others *(page 333)*

high priest
a powerful leader of the Temple at the time of Jesus *(page 175)*

holy
one of the four marks, or qualities, of the Church that show its truth and its origin in God. The Church is holy because we draw our life from God and offer people the way to God *(page 332)*

holy days of obligation
the six special days celebrated by the Church in the United States *(page 344)*

Holy Orders
the sacrament of commitment in which bishops, priests, and deacons are ordained to serve the Church in a special way *(page 337)*

Holy Spirit
the Third Person of the Trinity who leads and guides us in living as followers of Jesus *(page 331)*

honor
to treat with respect *(page 123)*

Immaculate Conception
the belief that Mary, the mother of Jesus, was conceived without original sin *(page 332)*

in vain
in a disrespectful way*(page 115)*

Incarnation
our belief that God became man in Jesus *(page 330)*

inheritance
the money and property received by a relative usually from someone who has died *(page 185)*

justice
loving God and all people by treating everyone fairly *(page 73)*

lay professionals
nonordained persons who work full time in the Church community *(page 351)*

Lent
forty days of preparation before Easter *(page 344)*

light of the world
the lives of Jesus and his followers shining before others and lighting the way to God and happiness *(page 235)*

liturgical year
the Church's official calendar of feasts and seasons *(page 344)*

Matrimony
another name for the sacrament of Marriage, in which a man and a woman promise to love one another for the rest of their lives as husband and wife *(page 337)*

meditation
using our imaginations instead of words to listen to God speaking to us *(page 352)*

mercy
loving care, or compassion *(page 83)*

Messiah
the title for Jesus as God's chosen one who would bring peace *(page 330)*

moral
a choice between right and wrong *(page 345)*

mortal sin
a very serious refusal to follow the teachings of Jesus, one which turns us away from God *(page 348)*

neighbor
every man, woman, and child, especially someone who needs our love and care *(page 63)*

obey
to do what someone who is responsible for you tells you to do *(page 123)*

one
one of the four marks, or qualities, of the Church that show its truth and its origin in God. The Church is one in our faith, sacraments, and leadership *(page 332)*

original sin
the first selfish act of the first human beings, and the sinful condition into which we are born *(page 25)*

peacemakers
people who try to bring peace and friendship where these things are needed *(page 83)*

Pentecost
the day the Church began with the coming of the Holy Spirit upon the first disciples. *(page 344)*

prayer
talking and listening to God *(page 352)*

reconciliation
making up through sorrow and forgiveness *(page 183)*

reign of God
the time when God's peace, love, and justice will rule our lives and the world *(page 73)*

respect
to act with care toward someone or something *(page 123)*

resurrection
Jesus' rising from death to new life *(page 330)*

reverence
an attitude of respect and care *(page 117)*

Sabbath
the weekly day of prayer and rest: Sunday for Christians, Saturday for Jews, and Friday for Muslims *(page 115)*

sacrament
a sacred sign that celebrates God's love for us and Jesus' presence in our lives and in the Church *(page 334)*

sacraments of healing
Reconciliation and Anointing of the Sick—the Church's two sacraments of healing *(page 336)*

sacraments of initiation
Baptism, Confirmation, and Eucharist—the Church's three sacraments of welcome and belonging *(page 334)*

sacrament of Reconciliation
the sacrament of healing that celebrates God's pardon and forgiveness of our sins *(page 336)*

saint
someone the Church singles out as an outstanding model of what it means to be like Jesus *(page 333)*

Samaritan
someone from Samaria, the land north of Jerusalem *(page 67)*

Savior
Jesus Christ, who brought us God's mercy and forgiveness and freed us from sin *(page 330)*

service
work that helps others who need our care *(page 243)*

shalom
the Hebrew word for peace, wholeness, well-being, and freedom from violence *(page 87)*

sin
to choose to act selfishly; to turn away from God and choose not to love; to fail to do something we know we should do *(page 37)*

Temple
the sacred house of worship for the Jewish people, which was located in Jerusalem *(page 67)*

temptation
an attraction to think, say, or do something we know is wrong *(page 33)*

Ten Commandments, the
the ten special rules given to us by God to help us live good lives *(page 93)*

values
what people consider important *(page 115)*

venial sin
a less serious act of selfishness, one which weakens our relationship with God *(page 348)*

violence
rough or harmful actions or words *(page 133)*

vocation
a calling from God to live in a way that allows each of us to serve others in the Christian community and in the world *(page 349)*

worship
giving honor and praise to God *(page 334)*

wholeness
being a complete person; having peace, faith, acceptance, and wellness *(page 87)*

Works of Mercy
the loving acts described in Matthew 25:31–46 that tell us how to respond to the basic needs of all people *(page 347)*

Index